WITCHES, GIANTS AND A GHOST CAT

Nina Dodd, Author • Asia Wetherell, Illustrator

A THANK YOU FROM THE AUTHOR

I would like to thank all the past and present Dunsterians who came forward with their stories and by doing so enabled these stories to be recorded and published for all to enjoy. I would also like to thank author Brian Hoggard for fact-checking my research on the British superstitions, Dunster Museum for providing information about local history, Asia Wetherell for the fabulously quirky collages, and editor Angela Jones and Jane Hunt for proof-reading the final drafts of the book. A massive thank you also goes to my husband Andrew, my beloved sons Alex and Nico, and all my friends and family, who bore through months and months of me talking of nothing but ghosts, protection marks, and the mystery tales of Dunster.

First published in Great Britain in 2023 by:

Dunster Books
30 High Street
Dunster, Somerset
TA24 6SG
United Kingdom
www.dunsterbooks.com

First Edition September 2023

Printed in Great Britain

ISBN 978-1-7395369-0-9

CONTENTS

FOREWORD

A village like Dunster, where the oldest buildings date back over 800 years, has had a multitude of inhabitants pass through, with world views that differ massively from our 21st century ones. Finding buried cats, witch bottles and scissors hidden inside the house walls, ceilings, floors and chimneys, and carved and burned protection marks on doors and fireplaces, may seem odd to us. However, for centuries, these were common practice in British people's desperate attempt to survive and make sense of a world where the origin of illnesses was not understood, no proper cures available and one bad crop could mean starvation. Life was unpredictable, and often incomprehensible.

The little scientific knowledge there was of the world, was not accessible to common people, most of whom were illiterate up until the latter half of the 1800s. It's no wonder then, that people in Britain sought help from amulets, magic potions, verbal charms, and protection marks - and toad-doctors, charmers, healers, and practitioners of magic - the *cunning-folk*, were in high demand.

In the centuries before television, newspapers and books were readily available to common Britons, the retelling of stories was one of the main means of not only passing on news and information, but also of entertaining people, whose lives consisted of long working days and very little free time. In tight knit communities like that of Dunster's, the stories, no doubt contained much gossip, but also useful information helping the villagers in the everyday running of their households, farms and businesses.

The more thrilling stories doing the rounds in medieval towns like Dunster (as it was referred to up until the first half of the 1800s, instead of a village) were often derived from tales told by travelling thespians, poets, storytellers and singers. These stories talked of court scandals, romantic affairs and bravery on battle fields;

but also of grizzly executions, ghosts, evil spirits, and the harm done by malicious fairies, pixies and witches.

While a number of the stories retold in this book derive from centuries ago, a good many of them are first-hand accounts told to the author by the former, and present-day 'Dunsterians'. Told by people, who firmly believe that their sensitivity makes them perceptible to encounters with spirits.

Even though some surveys show that nearly half of Britons believe in ghosts, there is still a stigma attached to those who speak of their other-worldly experiences. While the stories are willingly shared with the like-minded, and their nearest and dearest, public recounting of the encounters unnerves many. These recent stories, however, if not recorded, could be lost forever, resulting in future generations, and researchers, missing out on information on what people believed in villages like Dunster in the 21st century.

Owing to many of the stories being told of encounters in private homes, I have omitted the names of the interviewees, and the exact addresses of the buildings, except in cases where the present-day owners were happy to share them with the readers.

The book has been written with a dual purpose in mind, and therefore can be read as a collection of stories, local history and intriguing superstitions, or as a walking guide to the beautiful, yet at times spine-chilling, village of Dunster.

I hope you enjoy reading the book as much as I have writing it – and can still have a good night's sleep while staying in Dunster - even if you are woken up by the sound of a phantom army walking through your room or the White Lady standing by your bed.

Nina Dodd

The Prince of Wales, later to become King Charles II, stayed at the Dunster Castle in 1645.

CHAPTER 1
A BRIEF HISTORY OF DUNSTER

PREHISTORY (BEFORE 43 AD)

SACRED TREES AND THE DISCOVERY OF 2,000 YEAR OLD COINS

In order to appreciate the wealth of history a small village like Dunster hides behind its pretty facade, it is good to have a brief look at the events, superstitions and beliefs that moulded people's lives in different centuries. So, bear with this chapter, even if traditional history writing may normally send you to sleep.

Dunster's history started long before the building of the castle and the centuries old houses. The first signs of humans in the Dunster area - flint scatters found at nearby Alcombe and animal bones in Dunster's Park Street - are believed to possibly date back as far as 6,000-8,000 years ago. By the Iron Age (c. 800 BC — 1st century AD), there is evidence of the early inhabitants living on the hilltops surrounding the present-day Dunster village, and of growing crops, keeping animals - and, undoubtedly, worshipping gods and deities linked to nature.

Many of the written accounts of the beliefs of the early tribes of the British Isles come from Roman sources, dating after the year 43AD, when the Roman Conquest of Britain began. Even though modern historians recognise that the Roman writers may have been biased, they have managed to reconstruct a picture of a religious life where *druids* (shamanic priests and priestesses), performed animal - and possibly human - sacrifices, interpreted future events, acted as healers and judges, and were able to read and write. From the amount of Iron Age weapons, tools and decorated metalwork found in rivers and lakes around Britain, it is believed that sacrifices to the gods also included the depositing of valuables in sacred springs, rivers and groves.

The ancient tribes are believed to have worshipped sacred trees; oak, ash and yew, the latter of which can be found in many old churchyards across Britain. The oldest yews, estimated to be 2,000-5,000 years old, predate the churchyards they stand on, and are believed in some cases to have been part of ancient pagan sites of worship. The remains of one such ancient yew tree can also be found at Dunster's St George's churchyard.

Iron Age tribes were led by chieftains, who protected the inhabitants of their hilltop forts and the surrounding areas from rival tribes. There are traces of several such hill forts in the Dunster area, the largest being Bat's Castle, which sits on top of a ridge above Gallox Hill to the south of the present-day Dunster village. These two stone embankments consist of a circular area of approximately 1.2 hectares (3 acres) and are on the same spot where in 1983 two schoolboys found a hoard of ancient coins. The coins were later verified to date between 102 BC and 350 AD.

The steep path to Bat's Castle is clearly signposted from the east side of Dunster's Gallox Bridge and takes 30-60 minutes to reach by foot – depending on each individual's fitness levels. Once on the top, the views to the Avill Valley, and the Bristol Channel make the steep climb worthwhile, even for those who are not overly keen on history.

Here you may also run into one of the Exmoor Pony herds - a breed that is believed to have roamed free on Exmoor's hills for thousands of years.

ROMAN RULE
(43 AD – 410 AD)

PERHAPS THE ROMANS WERE HERE AFTER ALL?

Until recently, it was generally believed that the Romans only had a few small forts on the coast of the Bristol Channel, but did not venture properly into Exmoor. Recent discoveries in Dunster have, however, been changing that view.

The British *Time Team*, consisting of various historians, archaeologists and related professionals, uncovered fragments of Roman-age pottery in the gardens of Dunster's Park Street and High Street in the 2010s, and in 2015 a high tide exposed pieces of Roman pottery at Dunster Beach. This has led to speculation that there may have been a Roman-British settlement on the beach, and possibly a Roman port.

Romans introduced many improvements to the lives of the south-west Britons during their reign. They built roads and aqueducts, introduced toilets, bathrooms and new fruit trees such as pears and apples, without which the famous Somerset cider might never have been developed.

Even though the Romans destroyed many of the druid strongholds, built their own temples and banned druidism in 54 AD, they were believed to have been relatively tolerant towards native beliefs, just as long as the Imperial Cult - the worship of the Roman emperor as a god - was incorporated into their religious practices. What might have helped with the transition was that there was no massive clash in belief systems, as both the Romans and the Iron Age Britons believed in a pantheon of gods and spirits.

The Romans also believed in the power of good luck charms such as amulets, pendants and wind chimes, which were hung from doorways and windows, and believed to ward off evil spirits - much in the same way as amulets and charms were used by the English people during the following centuries.

When Christianity gained popularity in 4th century England, after Emperor Constantine's conversion, the pagan traditions and Christianity lived side by side. It is believed that in the private religious lives of the English people, belief in the old Celtic gods persisted.

EARLY MIDDLE AGES
(410 AD - 1066 AD)

THE END OF THE ELF RULER

After the Roman armies left Britain in 410 AD, various Northern European tribes, later to be called Anglo-Saxons, gradually took control of most of England, some by peaceful settlements, some by battles. It is believed that the Anglo-Saxons arrived in West Somerset, and Dunster, around 700 AD.

Some believe that there may have been a Saxon fortress on the hill where Dunster Castle is located now, even though there is not much hard evidence to support this. The Britons that lived in the south-west, and did not succumb to Anglo-Saxon rule, were believed to have been pushed further to the west, to what is now Cornwall, and to Wales.

Anglo-Saxons brought with them their own pantheon of North European gods, but eventually converted to Christianity. Anglo-Saxon Christianity, however, preserved many old pagan practices. Potions, verbal charms, certain stones and jewels, and the writing of Old English words, runes and symbols on objects, are believed to have been used to ward off evil spirits and illnesses. Belief in elves, giants, spirits and shape shifters is also assumed to have been common.

From the end of the 8th century AD, Vikings raided Britain and eventually established their rule in most of the north and east of England.

The shores surrounding Dunster did not escape the attacks from various Viking groups ransacking the Bristol Channel either. There are records of raids on Carhampton, the nearest major settlement to Dunster, and on Porlock and Watchet. Kitswall, on the coast between Dunster and Carhampton, is also believed by some to have been the site of a battle between the Vikings and Anglo-Saxons in the 9th century, led by King Egbert of Wessex.

Anglo-Saxon rule in Britain ended with the Norman Invasion of 1066. The fate of the last Saxon lord of Dunster, *Aelfric* (meaning the "elf ruler"), is not known, but as his land was given to a Norman nobleman, it is possible that Aelfric met his end in one of the battles against the new invaders.

MEDIEVAL PERIOD (1066-1485)

DUNSTER GROWS INTO AN IMPORTANT TOWN

The Normans, the descendants of the Viking settlers who held control of the northern parts of France, were the next invaders to rule England.

The Duke of Normandy, William the Conqueror, after defeating the Anglo-Saxons at the Battle of Hastings in 1066, brought in French speaking aristocracy, clergy and army, and divided the country up amongst his knights. One of these knights, William de Mohun, received around 70 manors in the south-west of England, including the manor of Dunster.

The first written reference to Dunster, or *Torre*, as it was called then, appears in the Domesday book of 1086 - a vast survey ordered by William the Conqueror to determine who-owned-what in conquered England and parts of Wales. This survey, which consists of two manuscripts and is held at the National Archives in London, mentions Dunster as having just 15 households and two mills at the time. Yet, when William de Mohun arrived in this small hamlet, he decided to make it his headquarters, and started the building work for his castle.

The first structure built by de Mohun is believed to have been a wooden fortress on the same hill where the present-day castle stands. Around the same time, building work on a new church and a priory started in Dunster.

With so much building being done, the population of the little hamlet grew rapidly. Carpenters and stonemasons moved in with their families, with merchants and artisans in their wake. The castle housed soldiers, and the Priory monks added to the number of new inhabitants.

By the end of the 12th century Dunster had grown so much that it was granted the status of a borough, and was later licensed to hold a weekly market, which quickly became the centre of the local economy. Many of the goods for the market were, no doubt, brought by sea via a port located at Dunster Beach, ships being amongst the easiest ways in medieval times to transport produce.

Religion played a massive part in the everyday lives of the medieval English. People from all walks of life would set off on pilgrimages, with some taking part in Crusades - the *'Holy Wars'* fought for various political and religious motives. Casualties were unavoidable and in 1193 William de Mohun IV died en route to Jerusalem on a mission to fight in the Third Crusade alongside King Richard, known as *'the Lionheart'*.

Other de Mohuns also played their part in affairs of state with several of them acting as Sheriffs of Somerset, responsible for collecting taxes and enforcing the law. The 1st Baron John Mohun, died after fighting at the Battle of Boroughbridge in the Barons' War, and John, the 2nd Baron, fought with Edward III at the Battle of Crécy. The latter was also one of the 25 founding knights of the Order of the Garter, and upon his death in 1375, was the last of the de Mohuns to own the Dunster estates.

In 1376 John's widow Joan sold the castle and manors to Elizabeth Luttrell, a transfer which resulted in the Luttrell family owning Dunster Castle until 1976, when Sir Walter Luttrell gifted the castle to the National Trust – a British charity founded in 1895 with a mission to protect historic buildings.

During the Middle Ages Dunster became an important town in the area with its own castle, priory, church, harbour, shops, mills, alehouses, vineyards and a market, which drew in buyers and sellers from the surrounding area.

On a national level, this period also saw the signing of Magna Carta, the Hundred Years War, The War of the Roses, devastating outbreaks of the plague, and the first witch trials.

Even though Catholicism was the official religion, old pagan beliefs and superstitions held their ground amongst all layers of society.

TUDORS & STUARTS (1485-1714)

THE WITCH CRAZE BEGINS

The Tudor dynasty (1485-1603) left its mark on history by producing a succession of unforgettable monarchs – Henry VIII, his eldest daughter Mary I (nicknamed *Bloody Mary* owing to her efficiency in executing the protestants who refused to convert to Catholicism), and Elizabeth I, the so-called Virgin Queen, viewed by some scholars as having been a kind of a Protestant substitute for the medieval Catholic Virgin Mary cult.

The English Civil War, the Monmouth Rebellion, wars with France, Scotland and Spain, religious conflict and periodic outbreaks of serious diseases such as plague, small pox, and the mysterious 'sweating sickness' meant that life was precarious for all classes of society, no matter where one lived.

In Dunster the cloth industry flourished, with evidence of cloth called 'Dunsters' being traded internationally. As an encouragement to trade, George Luttrell built the iconic Yarn Market in the High Street around 1609. He was also responsible for a major rebuilding of the Dunster Castle with much of the current building dating from that time.

It was also a period of great religious upheaval with Henry VIII starting the English Protestant Reformation in 1534. The dissolution of the monasteries (1536-1541) closed down all English monasteries, including Dunster's Benedictine priory. Over the following decades, most of Dunster's Priory lands were sold by the Crown to wealthy merchants and lawyers. The Luttrell family managed to secure the Priory buildings and some of the adjoining land, which became a farm and, later, a kitchen garden for the Dunster Castle. With the dissolution of the Benedictine priory, the whole of Dunster's St George's Church became available for the use of the townspeople again.

One might think that being far from the court would have kept Dunster away from its politics, but the Luttrell men, as with all nobility, were bound to serve the monarchs. Henry VII knighted Sir Hugh Luttrell in 1487 after the War of the Roses, and he was chosen to be one of the seven knights from Somerset to escort the Catholic queen-to-be, Catherine of Aragon, when she came to England in 1501 to marry Arthur - and later his younger brother Henry VIII. When England was building its naval force and expecting a Spanish attack, George Luttrell was given orders to build sea defences along the coastline in case the Spanish Armada attacked England through the Bristol Channel.

The biggest intrusion of national affairs into Dunster life, however, came in 1645, during the Civil War. The spring and early summer had already seen the town ravaged by the plague, and in the autumn of 1645 Colonel Blake and his parliamentary troops came to Dunster, intent on capturing the castle. The siege lasted for six months, disrupting the economy and causing damage to a number of buildings.

Dunsterians, like the rest of the common Britons, would have also felt pressure owing to the official state religion changing back and forth between Catholicism and Protestantism. The people who did not convert to the brand of Christianity the prevailing monarch was supporting, could - and did - face execution in England.

During this time the Church, and society as a whole, became obsessed with the Devil and its hold on the Britons, who, in spite of being devout Christians, held onto a massive amount of superstitions dating back to pagan days. In the war against evil spirits, an estimated 2,500-4,000 people were executed for witchcraft in the British Isles.

Dunsterians were as superstitious as the rest of the Britons. They buried cats and protective items in the walls and floors of their houses, and carved and burned protection marks wherever an evil force, they believed, could enter their homes.

18TH - 19TH CENTURIES

SHAMBLES AND SÉANCES

The 18th century was a relatively peaceful period in Somerset, even though it did see a decline in the economic prosperity of Dunster, and the South-West in general.

While England and Wales united with Scotland in 1707, and Britain grew into a strong trading nation with the help of the Industrial Revolution and colonisation, Dunster could not compete with the wool industry in the more industrialised English towns in the Midlands and Northern England. This resulted in many people moving from Dunster to other parts of England in search of work.

With the number of inhabitants declining, trade suffered and a number of unoccupied houses was reduced to ruins in Dunster. The row of market stalls located in the middle of Dunster's High Street, called *the Shambles*, fell into such disrepair that they were pulled down in the early 1800s.

A row of market stalls, called Shambles, were located in the middle of High Street until the beginning of the 1800s.

Even though the Luttrell family refurbished Dunster Castle and built the Conygar Tower, all of which created some employment in the town, jobs were scarce. Even Dunster market felt its popularity fading. On the corner of West Street and Mill Lane, an almshouse housed the poor from circa 1740 to 1834, after which the building was turned into a Victorian workhouse.

The main income for the Dunsterians in the 1800s came from various trades, agriculture and small businesses. The town was still self-sufficient with blacksmiths, tailors, dressmakers, saddlers, grocers, butchers and various tradespeople providing more or less everything the locals needed.

The 1800s saw St George's Church refurbished, new schools founded, and a hospital, new police station and Magistrates' Court built. A railway line was opened from Watchet to Minehead, and Dunster station built. Some of the houses in Dunster had new frontages built on top of their medieval walls.

The building works opened up new work opportunities, and brought in new settlers, resulting in the standard of living starting to rise again in Dunster. The census records show that during this period Dunster had a large influx of artisans and their families settling into the village.

Even though most Britons were Christians, superstitions and belief in the power of spirits - both good and bad - were still widespread in the 18th and 19th centuries. Belief in witchcraft and magic remained deeply rooted within the country folk of Somerset. Séances - meetings where a contact with the dead was attempted, usually via a medium - became the height of fashion in Britain, and were attended by Britons from all walks of life, including Queen Victoria herself.

With the invention of photography in 1839, spirit photography, i.e. photographers claiming to be able to capture ghostly apparitions on film, became a fad in Britain in the latter half of the 19th century, and the beginning of the 20th century. One of these early 20th century 'spirit photographs' is still hanging on the wall of Dunster's Luttrell Arms Hotel showing a tall woman standing in the window - a window, where the photographer swore no one was present when he took the photograph.

20TH - 21ST CENTURY

THE MAGIC OF DUNSTER

The nearby towns of Minehead and Watchet grew significantly in the early 20th century as a result of tourism and small-scale manufacturing industry. Dunster, however, remained very much an agricultural hub, with just a few hotels, tea-rooms and riding stables catering to tourists - mostly due to the Luttrells owning many of the business properties and houses, and having a great interest in preserving the historic feel of the town. Owing to this, Dunster escaped much of the 20th century rebuilding boom.

Many evacuees also found a refuge in Dunster during World War II, escaping the bombing in the cities - and staying on when the war ended. The list of the villagers who served in both World Wars is carved on a plaque at the Memorial Hall in the High Street.

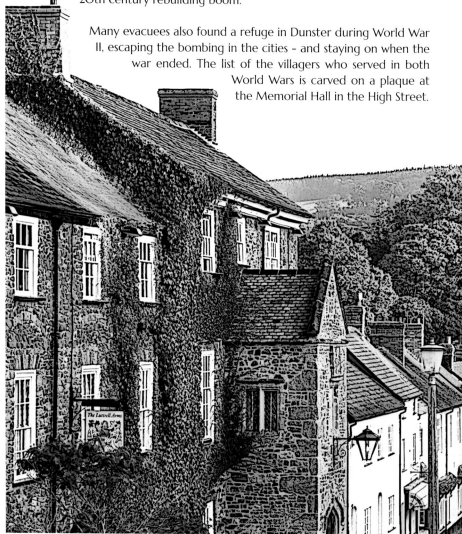

In 1951 much of the Dunster estate, including most of the houses the Luttrells owned, were sold, mainly to the existing tenants. The businesses listed in the sale catalogue included a smithy and a saddlery, a builder's yard and a coal merchant, a butcher, a tailor, two grocers and a chemist. With a newsagent and a post office, Dunster was still virtually self-sufficient in the middle of the 20th century.

Nowadays tourism is the main source of income for most of the businesses in Dunster with restaurants, tea rooms, hotels, holiday lets and shops catering to those who wish to experience the magic of Dunster. The village, as it is nowadays classed, rather than a town, has over 200 listed buildings, and is considered to be one of the best preserved, and most beautiful, medieval villages in the UK.

CHAPTER 2
ENGLISH SUPERSTITIONS

PROTECTION MARKS

Even though traditional history writing often concentrates on rulers, years of major events, wars, and politics, it is just as interesting to understand how the common people lived in villages and towns like Dunster - and how their beliefs and superstitions moulded society via the stories they shared.

In a society like that of Dunster's, where the commoners had no access to proper education until the 1800s, and people hardly left their hometowns, superstitions were understandably rampant. A lack of understanding of the origin of illnesses, and the strong belief in witches, ghosts, pixies, fairies, the Devil and other evil forces, resulted in people trying various methods to protect their homes and their families.

One of these protective methods in Dunster, as elsewhere in England, was the carving and scorching of *apotropaic* signs, more commonly known as PROTECTION MARKS, witch marks, or anti-witch marks, onto places in the houses, barns, churches, and public buildings, which were felt to be in the need of special protection.

By the middle of the 20th century, after the superstitions that resulted in the use of these marks had more or less died out in Britain, the researchers mainly viewed the marks as either decorative, graffiti, or carpenters' and stonemasons' marks - marks that would identify the maker of an object or structure. The research of recent years has, however, found that many of the marks were actually used for a specific purpose: to ward off evil.

The concept of evil spirits has been around since the dawn of time, but during the Middle Ages the Church, and society as a whole, became obsessed with the Devil. Evil was believed to be lurking everywhere, waiting to ruin, not just people's morals, but also their livelihoods and lives.

It was not just the Devil one was to be wary of; there were also witches, fairies, pixies, the undead revenants, and ghosts one should protect oneself, one's family, cattle, and home from. To keep evil out, protection marks were carved in Exmoor in places where the evil forces could enter: doors, window frames, fireplaces, and roof trusses. Such marks have also been found all around Britain, carved onto the walls next to beds, baby cradles and chests containing valuables.

There are many kinds of deliberately carved marks, many of which academic and layperson researchers are still to agree on whether to place them in the 'protection mark' category, or not. The marks, mostly agreed to be protection marks are the hexafoil/daisy wheel (a compass drawn circle with 4-6 petals, like the ones found inside Dunster's Tithe Barn), certain circles (believed by some to have originated as a solar symbol), pentagrams, mazes, and *merels* – an ancient board game – believed to hold protective qualities when found carved on walls.

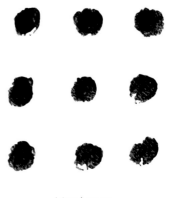

Merel game

Out of the carved letters, like the ones found inside Dunster's St George's Church, the overlapping V, M and VV are believed to be MARIAN MARKS, referring to the first letters of Virgin Mary, *Virgo Virginum*, who was an important object of worship in medieval England. The letters X and the triple crossed I (I being the first Greek letter in the word Jesus, *Iesus*) are, on the other hand, assumed to refer to Jesus Christ. In medieval times just inscribing the holy name of Christ, or the Virgin Mary, or carrying an amulet with a symbol representing these holiest of all Christian figures, was believed not just to ward off evil, but also to cure illnesses and bring general good luck.

Slightly more difficult protection marks to recognise are the MESH PATTERNS, also found in houses in Dunster, that quite often look like nothing but random, deep scratches. For centuries people believed that evil spirits and demons were attracted to lines, and when coming across one, would be compelled to follow it. As there is no end, the spirit would get trapped within the mesh, or a never-ending symbol such as a knot, and would not be able to cause harm to the surrounding areas, or people. This idea is believed by some researchers to stretch back to the sacred knots and puzzles of the early tribes inhabiting the British Isles, before the arrival of Christianity.

PROTECTION MARKS IN DUNSTER

The best known protection marks in Dunster can be seen inside the 16th century Tithe Barn. In the Middle Ages, people, besides paying taxes to their monarchs, were expected to pay one tenth of their earnings to the Church. These *tithes* were often paid in agricultural produce such as harvested grain and seeds. Much of the produce was kept in tithe barns - around 200 of which still survive in Britain.

Having such a valuable stock of produce, it is no wonder that Dunster's 16th century Tithe Barn had protective marks - daisywheels - moulded onto its walls. Unfortunately Dunster's Tithe Barn is only open to the public when there are events on, but if you can come on such a day, you will find the daisywheels on the interior wall of the main barn area.

The 12th century St George's Church also has a small collection of, what are believed to be, carved protection marks on the eastern end of the church. The defaced effigy of the Lord of Dunster Castle, Sir Hugh Luttrell, and his wife Catherine Beaumont, has crossed W letters, X marks, and compass circles carved onto it, all believed to be protection marks - made either to protect the Luttrells, or to take a little piece of the effigy from. Protective and curative potions could then be made out of the collected stone powder, as was customary in The Middle Ages.

Dunster's Tithe Barn

On the same effigy there is a carving of a house on the cheek of Lady Beaumont. When medieval Britons carved houses, boats or ships in churches, it is believed, it was to acquire sacred protection for the thing depicted - in this case, possibly, for the home of the person who did the carving.

There is also a merel board carved onto the stone slab with Lady Elizabeth Luttrell's figure on it, and a pentagram and Marian W marks, on and around Sir Thomas Luttrell's effigy.

The inhabitants of the private houses in Dunster have also made interesting discoveries in their homes: multiple X marks on an outside door latch, Marian marks and daisy wheels on window sills and roof trusses, mesh patterns, and masses of burn marks on the lintels of medieval fireplaces.

Besides carved marks, the historians doing research on protection marks, agree that BURN MARKS were commonly used for protection. These deliberate marks were made by holding a flame against a timber, and scraping away the carbon until a deep tear shaped mark was formed. One theory is that these marks were made to protect the buildings and objects against fire and lightning.

One of the buildings where you can see such burn marks is the business premises located at 24a High Street. The lintel on top of a large fire place, clearly visible when you walk into the premises, has several burn marks on it. There is also at least one burn mark inside St George's Church, on a 13th century chest used to store church valuables in, nowadays located next to the Sir Thomas Luttrell's effigy.

The place where you can find a much greater number of protective burn marks, however, is the wooden wall separating the Luttrell Arms Hotel's guest lounge and the entrance corridor. Besides the faint outlines of ships, the wall has over 20 burn marks believed to have been made deliberately for protective use.

When there are so many marks found in one place, a question does arise as to why this space was felt in the past to be in need of so much protection. Interestingly the room is the same one where some modern-day stories stem from, of hotel guests having encountered an apparition of an old woman sitting by the fire. The Luttrell Arms bar area next to the guest lounge also has a burn mark on the old door leading onto a passage joining the street and the quaint courtyard.

WITCH BOTTLES & HIDDEN SHOES

A nother object, found to have been used up until the 20th century as a protection for buildings, and their inhabitants, was a SHOE. Found in great numbers hidden under floors, around doors, above ceilings, and in the chimneys of old Somerset and British homes, public houses and churches, the correlation between a shoe and a belief in its protective powers, is perhaps a bit harder to grasp. Nearly half of the recorded concealed shoe finds in Britain do not date to the Middle Ages, but to the 1800s, meaning that the belief in the protective qualities of a shoe held strong in the minds of many British people for centuries.

Some researchers believe that shoes were connected to witches, who were supposed to be attracted to them due to the scent of a human. Once entering the shoe, the witch, it was said, would not be able to reverse, and would be trapped inside the shoe hence not being able to cause damage to the dwellers of the building.

As shoes also take the unique shape of the wearer's foot they may have been used as a decoy for the person. The shoes, most of the concealed ones found being heavily worn, were hidden in the structures of houses and in the chimneys, where they would become targets for any evil forces trying to enter the dwellings. The hiding of shoes could also be related to the belief that the way to get rid of a domestic fairy, was to gift it with a piece of clothing, or shoes.

It is quite common in centuries–old houses like the ones in Dunster, for the owners, when doing renovations, to find odd objects buried onto the walls, ceilings, floors and fireplaces of their properties. For centuries it was believed that witches, evil spirits, fairies and pixies hated objects made of iron, and therefore metal objects can be found hidden in the structures of the houses, especially around doorways, to ensure that no evil could pass through.

Vessels such as stoneware Bellarmine drinking jugs and glass bottles were used as witch bottles.

When the ceiling of the 17th century shop premises on 30 High Street was renovated in 2022, a pair of old scissors was found hidden above the door, and next to it, a small glass bottle. Whether or not the purpose of the scissors was to keep the iron-hating evil spirits out, and the bottle to act as what is described by researchers as a witch bottle, is unclear, but hiding such objects was common in England all the way to the 19th, and even 20th century.

The WITCH BOTTLES were commonly sold by the local Somerset practitioners of folk medicine and magic, often referred to as the *cunning folk*, to people who wished to protect their homes, or to cure the inhabitant of the house of bewitchment. The bottle was instructed to be buried in the ground, under a hearthstone, boiled on a fire, or hidden in the structures of a house. These bottles, as research has found, often contained urine, human or animal hair, sharp objects such as pins, nails or thorns, pierced leather hearts or paper with writing and symbols on.

If a house or its inhabitants were in need of protection, the cunning folk in Somerset could also suggest taking the heart of an animal, such as that of an oxen's, pierce it with nails and hang it inside the chimney. The person sending a spell or an ill-wish to the household, would then experience great discomfort himself, or herself, when coming across the heart, or a witch bottle, and in order to cure himself, would be forced to undo the spell.

As academic research into concealed objects is still fairly new, and the general public and the builders renovating the houses have not been aware of what these finds actually are, many of these historic objects found in the walls of the houses have unfortunately been disposed of.

The most repulsive objects to modern day inhabitants, when found in their own houses, such as MUMMIFIED CATS, sometimes found placed alongside mummified mice, birds, animal skulls or witch bottles, have understandably been disposed of quickly. Unlike dead animals found trapped inside the structures of the buildings and dying due to not being to get out, the concealed, protective animals can often be found in staged poses, with reared backs, hissing or attacking a mummified rat or a mouse. Research has also found that some of these concealed cats were bought as skeletons with a skin–like covering and then placed inside the structures of the buildings.

Cats, like the one found buried under the stairs in one of Dunster's Church Street houses, have a long history associating them with gods and other-worldly abilities such as a sixth sense. Perhaps for this reason the placing of dead cats in the structures of English houses was thought to be effective, the thinking behind it possibly being that with these psychic abilities, the cat could find and rid the house of evil spirits.

AMULETS AND A DEAD MAN'S HAND

IN THE MIDDLE AGES, even though the Church tried to root out widespread superstitions, it is believed that many of the church officials themselves were just as superstitious as the commoners.

In an era when pilgrimages to famous churches were customary, these churches made the most of the footfall by selling amulets and *'pilgrim souvenirs'* to the masses of believers, who came seeking forgiveness for their sins, or a cure for illnesses.

If the church was fortunate enough to have managed to obtain a sacred artefact, such as a body part of a saint, a piece of what was claimed to be a splinter of Christ's cross, or a holy well believed to cure illnesses, the money obtained from the sale of the amulets meant that the clergy's daily bread was secured.

These amulets comprised various evil and illness repellants, such as pieces of holy scriptures, drawings of Christian symbols or daisywheels, and even small bottles that the clergy and monks claimed to contain saints' (such as the murdered archbishop, Thomas Becket's) blood. The amulets could be worn as necklaces, rings, or badges attached to hats and clothing.

When the protestant Reformation swept across Britain, amulet sales by the Church were no longer encouraged by the royal rulers, or by the top officials of the Church. The producing of amulets, however, did not cease amongst folk healers and quack doctors. When the educated doctors could not heal the patients, which seems to have happened more often than not, the common folk, who may not have been able to afford the services of the doctors, turned to the local magical practitioners for help.

The cures described were in many cases used much like amulets. A toad doctor in Somerset could, for example, advise a patient to carry a bag around his neck, containing toads' legs, cut

off from a live animal, baked, and ground to powder with a pestle and mortar. Other examples of the old amulets found in the West Country include a jaw bone of a black dog and parchments with symbols drawn on. The most precious amulets, such as the ones used to ward off fevers, toothaches, and snake bites could be handed down from one generation to the next, and often, in order for the amulet to sustain its power, it was said, had to be given on to a member of the opposite sex. A *Western Times* newspaper from 1909 mentions that such *"white witching"* used to be common in Dunster.

TRANSFERENCE

Many protective and curative objects in the Middle Ages derived from the common belief in *'transference'.* It was believed that if a person suffering from a disease, or ill-fortune, managed to transfer the misfortune to another person, or an animal, it would rid the person of the ailment.

Amongst the most powerful objects were the ones associated with EXECUTIONS. A piece of a rope used for hanging, or a cut off, executed person's hand were believed to cure illnesses, just by touching them on the patient's body. The illness was believed to go to the hand, or to the rope, and the convicted, dead person would take the illness with him to hell. It is also said that some nurses in the Middle Ages would bring children to be stroked with hands of the executed criminals, sometimes while the wretched convicts were still writhing on the end of the rope.

Prisoners being led to the gallows were also commonly touched by the townspeople gathered around the streets to watch the processions. This touching is believed to have been a similar form of transference, i.e. transferring the illnesses from the townspeople onto the prisoners to be executed.

Even though executed body parts were believed to be especially powerful, there is evidence of people using the touch of hands of other dead people as well for cures. A West

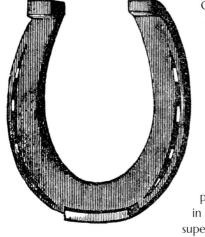

Country text from 1564 talks of the touch of an ordinary man's hand, while intact on his dead body, being used to cure cysts, boils and ulcers. The same logic included the use of many other objects, such as rubbing a wart with a snail or touching a rock, and leaving it in a place where an unsuspecting passer-by might pick it up, and in so doing, pass the illness to that person.

Dead bodies were believed to contain powerful cures against illnesses in general in medieval times, and not just amongst the superstitious common folk. A story tells that Queen Mary, William III and Charles II, the latter of whom, while staying at Dunster Castle in 1645 as a young prince is said to have encountered a ghost, were given a potion containing grated human skull. Blood, fat and human sweat were also used as cures for various illnesses.

Other protective amulets in the south-west, as in other parts of England, included horseshoes nailed onto doors, horse brasses, and iron objects that were believed to ward off anything from evil spirits to witches, pixies and fairies.

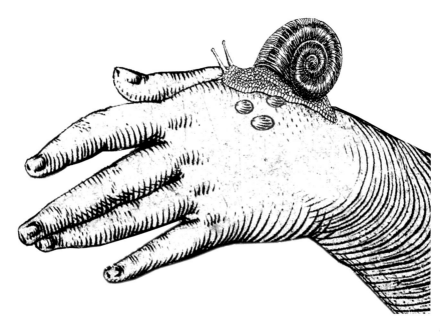

OTHER COMMON ENGLISH SUPERSTITIONS

I t is said that before modern science became the official worldview of the western world, nearly every object people encountered in their daily lives had superstitions associated with it. So was the case in Exmoor as well.

FIREPLACES were the centre of every household in England, and the chimneys - which became more common from the 16th and 17th centuries onwards - leading to them being one of the main passageways believed to be vulnerable to the access of evil forces. Besides hiding protective objects such as animal hearts, shoes and witch bottles, and carving, or burning, protective marks onto the mantlepieces, large fireplaces are reported to have been used by the local cunning folk, and wise women to perform their magic in. A description in F.J. Snell's *A Book of Exmoor* from 1903 describes how a wise woman would stand inside a fireplace, and while gazing up into the heavens, would incant her spells aimed at removing what was ailing the household. Chimneys were strongly associated with witches, and in many parts of England it was said that if the smoke from a fireplace was spilling out into the room, the reason was because a witch was sitting on the roof, blocking the chimney. The cure? Go outside and shoo the witch away.

When the literacy rate started increasing from the 1800s onwards, the **BIBLE** was not just used for reading scriptures, but also for fortune-telling in Somerset. The book would be laid on the table, opened at random, and the verse the reader's finger would be placed on, was read aloud. The rest of the family would then try to interpret what the meaning was. The Bible was also believed to be a mighty weapon against witchcraft, and if a bewitchment was suspected, it could be placed under the pillow to counteract the spell. Many of the verses from the Bible were also used in charms and counter-witchcraft rituals.

The belief in the power of a **HAG-STONE** - a stone with a hole created by water - was an enduring folk superstition for centuries in the West Country and elsewhere in England. These stones were believed to have powerful protective qualities to keep away a variety of illnesses, and to fight off spells and nightmares.

Hag-stones - also referred to as *'witch's stones'* - could be built into the walls, or hung on entrance ways to the houses and stables. When carried on one's person, they were also believed to give the owner the power to recognise a fairy or a witch - even when these creatures were disguised in an animal or human form.

It was believed that evil spirits were attracted to holes, but as they were too large to fit through them, they would get trapped inside, and therefore could not cause harm to people - or their farm animals. The holes in stones were believed to be especially powerful if created by moving water, as water was considered godly and pure, therefore being a natural repellant against evil forces.

Another practice related to the belief in the protective quality of HOLES is that of passing objects and persons through them. If parents wanted their child to be blessed with good luck or to grow to be strong, a custom in many parts of England was to pull the child through a hole carved into a big wheel of cheese or a large hole in a stone.

A split tree was also believed to hold similar, curative powers. After a child - or an adult - was passed through it, the tree would be bound back together. As the tree grew in strength, it was said, so would the person who had been pulled through it.

A *West Somerset Free Press* article from 1909 describes one of these West Country rituals where children born with a hernia were attempted to be cured by *"passing them naked through a cleft of ash at sunrise, on a Sunday morning, in a direction from east to west"*.

The belief in the EVIL EYE, or *'overlooking',* as it was referred to in England and in Somerset, was a serious worry for centuries. This superstition consisted of a belief that certain people could cast a curse on their fellow citizens simply by looking at them in a malevolent way. The people who were 'overlooked' would display varied symptoms such as low spirits and a lack of energy, which, in the worse cases, were believed to lead to death. The ways to protect oneself included spitting and crossing one's fingers, when a threat was suspected.

BREAKING A MIRROR is a superstition still widely associated with bad fortune, and predates many of the old English superstitions. In ancient Greece it was believed that a person's reflection was a representation of their soul, and if the reflection appeared distorted in water, a great disaster would strike. The Romans, on the other hand, believed that breaking a mirror would lead to seven years of bad luck. In medieval England people tried to wash away the bad fortune by placing the broken pieces in water, or leaving the mirror where it broke for seven hours, before taking it away.

BEES were much revered through the centuries in the West Country for their ability to produce heavenly sweet honey for consumption, and to make church candles out of. Bees were also believed to accompany the soul of the deceased to the other world, and therefore in the olden days in the West Country it was said to be a custom to inform the bees whenever a death occurred in the family. Otherwise, it was believed, the bees might also die. Bees were also told of the families' weddings and births, and food from the events was taken to the bees to keep them from vacating the precious hives.

ANIMALS were associated with an endless number of superstitions in the West Country. A bird trapped in the house, or tapping at a window, or a cock crowing at midnight was believed to foretell a death in the house, and a hen trying to crow to forecast serious ill–fortune. A cuckoo's cry would tell how many years of life one had left to live. Meeting a hare or a raven on the road was an especially ill omen, but meeting a toad on the road meant that something good was to happen. A kitten born in May was believed to bring vermin into the house.

THROWING COINS INTO WELLS is also believed to derive from ancient times, when bodies of water were believed to be the home to water deities, and offerings were thrown in to ensure good fortune. In England many valuable artefacts and swords have been found in rivers, along with pilgrims' amulets. During medieval times many of the sacred springs in Exmoor, Somerset and elsewhere in England became associated with Christian saints, and people did not only drink the water, but would also give offerings to the saint, often in the form of coins.

SNEEZING in the Middle Ages was a serious business. Illnesses were rife, but people also believed that when a person opened his mouth wide, the Devil could enter the body - or worse still, if he sneezed especially hard, he might sneeze out his soul. Saying *"God bless you"* was used as a spoken charm, a charm that is still used in Britain, in a shorter form. One of the West Country beliefs also talks of the dangers of when and how many times one sneezes. Sneezing once before breakfast would make one's day lucky, but if the sneezing happened on Monday or Friday, a disaster was bound to happen.

A belief in the healing power of the **SEVENTH SON** and the **SEVENTH DAUGHTER** of a family is believed to have been particularly rife in Exmoor. It was believed that by just touching such a person one could heal the diseases ailing them. A newspaper article from 1870 describes how mothers in the West Country would still in the 19th century bring their babies to be touched by the seventh children of families in the hope of curing illnesses. It was also commonly advised that seventh sons, due to their inherent abilities in curing illnesses, should train in medicine.

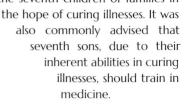

A belief in **UNLUCKY DREAMS** was another peculiar West Country superstition. To dream of a clergyman in a church, a copper penny or eggs, was believed to be especially unlucky. On the contrary, if a maiden dreamt of a funeral three times in a row, it was said, she would not become an old maid.

It is told that some old West Country women in the 1800s claimed that by just **HEARING THE CHURCH BELLS** chime, they could tell from the tone of the bells, if the next death in the village would be soon. The women would stand in the village streets, cupping their ears with their hands to catch the sound better, and scaring the passers-by just by looking at them knowingly.

The *Bristol Mercury* from June 1889 also mentions that in some Somerset churches the church clock had to be stopped during services. This was because it was believed that if the church clock struck while the congregation was singing a hymn, one of the parishioners would die within a week.

FOLKTALES AND
DUNSTER'S BELOVED GIANT

Exmoor has a great number of folktales, which were passed on orally from one generation to the next. Like elsewhere in England, the ever-evolving tales talked of magic beings, heroes and villains, and served many functions - from providing entertainment, to teaching important morals to the listeners. Pixies and fairies were amongst the most popular topics of Exmoor folktales, as were the tales of the Devil's adventures in the area. There is even a folktale about King Arthur and St Carantoc subduing a dragon tormenting Dunster!

One of the most charming Exmoor folktales, based in Dunster, tells a story of a giant who was said to have lived on the Grabbist Hill, located on the west side of Dunster. Born in Cornwall, this good-natured giant, as one of the variations of the tale goes, decided to move to Exmoor to escape his badly-behaved cousins. When the giant arrived in Dunster, the townspeople were terrified, but as time went on, and they realised that there was nothing to be afraid of, they became very fond of him.

The giant was not interested in human flesh or the locals' cattle, but was said to feed on the fish he caught in great numbers from the Bristol Channel. The giant was renowned for being so accomplished in finding fish, that local fishing boats would follow him, and by doing so, secured bountiful catches.

The giant was also loved for helping out the local humans. One day when a storm hit one of the fishing boats, filled with fish, and in danger of sinking, the giant is said to have picked the ship out of the water and delivered it to Watchet harbour. Every time the giant would return from his fishing trips, he would sit down on Grabbist Hill and wash his muddy feet in the River Avill. The townspeople would then wave at the giant, and when they got him to wave back, the charming story goes, their washing was dried in no time.

Whether this giant is the same one appearing in another folktale told of a competition between the Devil and a giant, is not known, but the setting of the competition is based in close proximity to Dunster. One of the variations of the folktale goes that the giant and the Devil decided that Exmoor was not big enough for both of them, and decided to settle the matter with a competition, the loser of which would have to leave the area. They met up at Hurlstone Point, on the side of Bossington Hill, located just over six kilometres from Dunster. The competition was about who could throw a large stone over to nearby Porlock Common. The Devil's stone landed perfectly on the common, and was left standing upright. When it was the giant's turn, the Devil, fearing he might lose the competition, coughed just as the stone was about to leave the giant's mighty hands, making the stone land short of the Devil's. The giant, being much bigger than the Devil, pushed the Devil on the ground, sat on top of him, and lit his pipe, totally ignoring the Devil whining under the giant's great weight.

Once he finished smoking, the story goes, he emptied the ash on the Devil's head, and told him that he didn't think the competition had been fair. The giant then promised a rematch on the Quantocks, took the Devil by his tail, and threw him into Porlock Bay, to cool down his anger and his head, covered in hot ash.

PIXIES AND FAIRIES

I t is believed that nearly every village and town in England had rocks, trees, springs and hills associated with tales of fairies and pixies in the Middle Ages, and centuries afterwards. Anglo-Saxons' Iron Age hill forts, burrows, and standing stones were particularly closely associated with stories of the *'little people'* or *'good neighbours'*, as pixies and fairies were often referred to as.

One of the fears associated with the folktales told of pixies in the vast open spaces of Exmoor, was to be *pixy-led* in the night, often by following lights carried by the little people, and ending up getting lost until daylight released the traveller from the spell. If nothing else, this certainly made a good excuse for husbands arriving back to their wives in the early hours of the morning, after an evening spent at the local alehouses - of which there were plenty in Dunster.

Besides husbands perhaps using the little people as an excuse for their late night shenanigans, it is also believed that the smugglers and other criminals operating in Exmoor may have used the stories of fairies and pixies to keep the locals, and travellers, away from areas where they conducted their illicit business.

The green-clad, red-headed Exmoor pixies were said to also have loved playing tricks on people, like blowing out lanterns and candles - especially on those who dared to wander into the dark woods, and desolate hills, where the little people were said to have felt most at home.

Both pixies and Exmoor fairies were also said to love dancing, but if a human was to stumble upon one of these gatherings, he was to take great care. The little people were renowned for guiding people through perilous bogs, woods and waters, if one was to follow the processions.

The pixies were also feared for stealing human children, much in the same way as fairies. The *"away with the fairies"* saying comes from exactly this, of humans, both adults and children, believed to have been either stolen by the fairies, or behaving in a strange way. Children that started displaying symptoms of physical or mental disability - or exceptional intelligence - and the adults behaving in an uncommon way to their previous selves, could be suspected of being CHANGELINGS.

For centuries it was believed that fairies could take a human, and leave in his, or her, place one of their own. The way to test if the person actually was a changeling included holding them near a fire and tricking them into holding iron scissors, which were believed to burn the skin of pixies and fairies. The fairies would then

feel that one of their own was in danger and bring back the original child, or the adult. Testing was rather dangerous, though, and there were reported deaths where children and adults were forcibly placed so close to the fire that their clothes were set on fire.

Many a tale was also told of humans wandering too close to the renowned entry points to the fairy world, and not reappearing until decades later. Time in the fairy world was believed to go much slower than in the human one, and what might have seemed like a few hours, or days, to the spellbound, so it was said, actually could have been decades in the human world. When the abductee finally managed to escape back to the human world, he might find all his loved ones having died of old age.

Not all the tales told of pixies and fairies were bad ones, though, as the little people were also renowned for helping humans. They could do chores in human homes, field work, or even lead a mean husband to meet his end in one of Exmoor's bogs, that way freeing the family of their misery. In return the humans would leave out

milk, bread and meat, or fresh water and soap for the little people to wash themselves with.

The way to protect oneself from fairies and pixies, besides taking care while wandering in the Exmoor woods and hills, was to carry a piece of an iron object on one's person, and hiding iron objects near the entryways to one's home. Wearing clothes or gloves inside out was also supposed to annoy fairies and pixies, hence forcing them to either keep their distance from humans, or to break the spell already cast on them. Other protection methods included making a criss-cross pattern on the malt when brewing ale, never wearing green in May and keeping a pin in a baby's dress until christening.

During the witch hunts in Britain, some of the unfortunate men and women suspected of being witches, also told tales, often under torture, of them learning their skills from, not just the Devil, but from fairies and pixies.

Many of the old Exmoor place names such as Pixie Rocks, Pixie Lane, and Pixie Meadow refer to these centuries old folktales. Dunster Castle also has its own well pool named Pixie Well.

WITCHES

A more sinister side of the common superstitions from the Middle Ages until the 1800s, was the belief in the evils of witchcraft, and the constant presence of the Devil waiting to lead God-fearing citizens astray.

Before the Church waged a full-blown war on witches in Britain in the 1500s, the seers, healers, herbalists, and fortune tellers were often revered, and much needed, members of society.

Since the arrival of Christianity on the British Isles the Church had been trying to stamp out folk superstitions, and the power the healers and the wise wives held in society. However, the real turning point came in 1589, when King James VI of Scotland, later to become King James I of England after the death of Elizabeth I, became convinced that the storm that nearly sank the ship carrying him and his bride Anne, was summoned by witches.

James set up his own tribunal which escalated into a devastating surge of witch trials on the British Isles, during which an estimated 2,500-4,000 men and women were executed, or killed as a result of witch-mobbings. Unlike the European continent where witches were burned, most executions in Britain were done by hanging.

Even though Somerset escaped the worst of the witch hunting craze, the belief in the harm done by supposed witches was rife. People would wear bells on their clothing, or carry onions in their pockets to keep witches away. If the cows did not produce a normal amount of milk, witches were blamed for sucking the milk out. If the butter or the cheese did not set properly, it was a witch's doing. If the fishermen setting off from harbours such as Minehead, Dunster and Watchet, did not get a good catch, the culprit, again, was a witch. Unusual and prolonged diseases were also blamed on witches. Even in the 1800s mental illnesses, epilepsy, cancer, heart disease and rheumatism were often seen as being caused by a witch's spell.

In tight-knit communities, like Dunster, with a small population, who generally did not travel outside of their own area, gossip and conflicts were commonplace. In such communities, anyone with an unusual appearance, bad temper, or too much beauty, could become the object of witchcraft accusations.

Contrary to the popular stereotypes of today, in past centuries both men and women could be accused of being witches. In Somerset and elsewhere in England, male witches were often referred to as wizards, and the act of bewitchment 'ill-wishing', or 'overlooking'.

The problem in trying to paint a picture of how many witch accusations there actually were involving Exmoor inhabitants is that the centuries old trail of records is not intact. What is known, though, is that the nearby towns of Taunton and Bridgwater had their own witch trials and executions in the 17th century.

THE WITCHCRAFT ACT OF 1735 put an end to the official prosecution of supposed witches in Britain. Instead, what became illegal was for people to pretend that they used magic. The last case of a Somerset dweller accused of being a witch took place in 1707, the case, fortunately, ending in acquittal.

Despite changing times, and the Witchcraft Act, the local magical practitioners, the *cunning folk*, were still making a good trade selling charms and performing counter witchcraft rituals in 19th century Somerset. Some cunning folk would travel from town to town offering their potions and services, but if there was not one available nearby, it was not unusual for the Somerset country folk to travel miles to bigger towns like Taunton and Bridgwater, to see one. Interestingly, a large number of the 19th century Somerset cunning folk were male.

SHAPE SHIFTING STORIES involving witches were widely told around Somerset. People believed for centuries that witches could take on any animal form, with the hare, the cat, and the toad being amongst the most common ones. The stories often followed the same pattern: while wandering around villages in a form of an animal, the witch would be attacked by a dog, or shot at, and found containing the same injuries in human form. Famous Exmoor shapeshifting witch stories included the 19th century Brendon-based Fanny Pope, Molly of Oare and Madam Carne of Sandhill - all of whom were said to have been able to turn themselves into hares.

FAMILIARS were animals believed to have been gifted to a witch by the Devil himself. They would act as companions to the witches, but also as spies, believed to have been sent out to the local communities to gather information, and to deliver spells. A familiar was believed to be able to appear in many forms, as cats, toads, hares, dogs, rats, owls, lambs, ferrets, or even as chickens. At the height of the witch craze just owning a suspiciously acting pet was a precarious business and could make the owner an object of witch accusations.

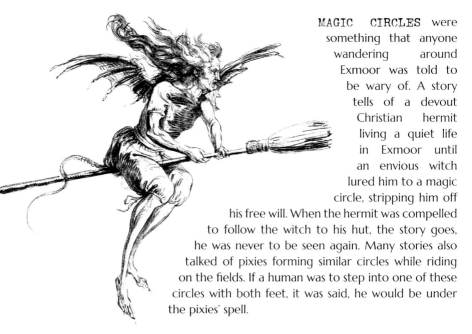

MAGIC CIRCLES were something that anyone wandering around Exmoor was told to be wary of. A story tells of a devout Christian hermit living a quiet life in Exmoor until an envious witch lured him to a magic circle, stripping him off his free will. When the hermit was compelled to follow the witch to his hut, the story goes, he was never to be seen again. Many stories also talked of pixies forming similar circles while riding on the fields. If a human was to step into one of these circles with both feet, it was said, he would be under the pixies' spell.

An act of WITCH SCRATCHING was believed to be an effective way to counteract a spell. The person suspected of being a witch, while minding his or her own business, would be attacked and scratched with a nail, or a needle, in order to draw blood. The blood was then collected, and smeared on the victim of the suspected spell. There are records of the witch scratchings ending up in courts still in 19th century Somerset, when the suspected witches demanded compensation for the injuries inflicted on them.

It was said that one way of telling who was a witch in the West Country was the way the person would behave INSIDE A CHURCH. It was believed that a witch might try to enter a church to make himself, or herself, appear as a regular God-fearing Christian, but could not face the altar or bow at the mention of God.

Another way for the local courts and communities around England, and Somerset, to try to identify a witch, was to use the infamous WITCH SWIMMING test, also called the 'trial by water'. The suspected witch was tied with a rope - sometimes to a chair - and placed in water. If he or she floated, there was no doubt of their guilt, as water, viewed as pure and Godly, was believed to reject the witch's unholy body. If the suspected witch sank, and survived the test, the charges were dropped.

Owing to earlier centuries' lack of scientific knowledge, and the slow progress of the knowledge filtering down to all the layers of the society when it finally was available, great many disorders were blamed on witches in England and the West Country even in the early 1900s.

One of these disorders, a sleep disturbance called **HAG-RIDING** was the dreaded state where a person, convinced of having been bewitched, would wake up in the middle of the night, and find himself unable to move. The incident often included a feeling of someone sitting, or riding on the victim's chest, and hallucinations of a threatening presence in the room. This condition is nowadays recognised as a medical condition called *sleep paralysis*.

OLD MOTHER LEAKEY

The belief that witches were behind storms, just as James VI of Scotland accused witches of nearly sinking the ship he and his bride were travelling on, can be found in many stories around the British Isles, including the famous local Exmoor tale of Old Mother Leakey, a woman described in some tales as a witch and in others as a ghost.

The real–life Susan Leakey was a woman who lived in Minehead in the 1600s. During Mrs Leakey's life she was considered to be a kind church–going person, yet, the tale goes, she was said to have warned her friends and family that this might not be the case once she died.

Shortly after Susan Leakey's burial, locals started telling stories of encounters with her in various locations in and around Minehead, on the beach, quay, at Dunster's St Leonard's well, and the hills and the fields surrounding Minehead.

One of her children, Alexander, the owner of several ships trading between Minehead and Ireland, was said to have been the continuous target of his deceased mother's wrath. The locals said that Mother Leakey was seen standing on Minehead quay, waiting for Alexander's ships to arrive. Once the ships came into view, Mother Leakey would blow a whistle, which would set off storms which caused great damage to the ships, even sinking some of them. This continuous misfortune eventually led Alexander's business to wither as it was said that no crew wanted to board his ships.

Mother Leakey was also said to have appeared in her old home, and, in the many tales told of her, even accused of killing her own grandson in his cradle (even though records show that the grandson, John Leakey, died at the age of 14). During one of these encounters, Alexander's wife Elizabeth, another witness of Old Mother Leakey's appearances, is said to have asked her mother-in-law why she kept on causing trouble to the family. The reply, the story goes, was that Mother Leakey had unfinished business which involved a golden necklace that she wanted her daughter-in-law living in Barnstaple to give back to her son Alexander. The more serious accusation involved her son-in-law, Bishop John Atherton, who she said had had an affair with her other daughter, an act classed as incest in the 1600s.

Word about these rumours also reached King Charles I who ordered his privy council to send three justices of the peace to investigate the claims. Even though many locals were said to have come forth as witnesses to the sightings of Mother Leakey, no hard evidence of the bishop's wrong-doings was found. However, in 1640, John Atherton was hanged after being found guilty of performing sodomy with his male servant, and Old Mother Leakey was said to have had her revenge.

GHOST STORIES

S tories of ghosts wandering with the living date back thousands of years, and have been told, and retold, around the world, from one generation to another.

Britain, however, is especially rife with stories of otherworldly encounters. According to some recent polls, nearly half of the British population believe in ghosts - and, while interviewing the local people living around Dunster and Exmoor, it seems that nearly every person either knows of someone who has had a spooky incident, or has had a first-hand encounter him or herself.

A view held by some visiting, and local, mediums is that Dunster is especially active in the ghost department. The stories recalled vary from sweet scents appearing from nowhere, to sounds of marching, and full-blown apparitions of monks, Roman soldiers and Grey and White Ladies. Most of the stories are not scary, but recount the amazement felt by the people witnessing the encounters.

The idea of what a ghost is, has changed several times over the centuries in Britain - and not just according to one's individual beliefs. In the early Middle Ages, the church viewed ghosts mainly as demons, but its view changed with the concept of *purgatory*. It was believed that when a person died, evil souls went directly to hell, pure souls to heaven, and the rest stayed in purgatory until they were purified, and then progressed to heaven. Purgatory was described as a place where souls were cleansed by an actual fire, and in medieval England, ghosts, called *revenants*, were seen by some as souls stuck in this stage.

In order to help these troubled souls to move on, the church developed complex rituals, including exorcism. According to F.J.Snell's *A Book of Exmoor,* such exorcism was also practised on Exmoor, with locals recounting that a parson needed to be especially strong to *'lay a ghost'* or otherwise his own health could suffer.

The Church also made a great amount of money by selling indulgences to their parishioners with a promise attached that by paying, they could shorten their time in purgatory. The corruption of the clergy, and the amount of money amassed through the selling of indulgences is believed to have been one of the catalysts resulting in the Reformation of the Church in England.

When the Reformation swept across the British Isles, and the concept of purgatory was omitted from Protestant theology, the folk belief in ghosts did not falter. Even though many of the stories described ghosts as murdered men and women, who came back to avenge their death, there were also stories of good ghosts, who came back to do chores in their old homes.

The 19th century saw another surge of interest in ghosts. Séances - meetings at which people attempted to make contact with the dead - were the height of fashion in Victorian England. Prestigious universities, such as Oxford and Cambridge, had their own ghost clubs dedicated to finding evidence of the existence of ghosts, and even Queen Victoria herself, is said to have attended such séances.

The many, blatantly fraudulent mediums of the 19th and 20th century, however, still affect the views people hold towards mediums in 21st century Britain. Even though some polls show that a great number of Britons believe in ghosts, many are hesitant to speak openly about their experiences owing to the fear of being ridiculed. Nowadays, ghosts are seen by many as troubled souls that have stayed with the living either owing to unfinished business, inability to let go of beloved people and places, or to such a sudden, accidental death that the deceased hasn't had time to realise his or her own passing.

Some 21st century Britons also believe that the energy of particularly strong people can be absorbed into the fabric of buildings, resulting in the repetitive actions of apparitions, such as walking through a room over and over again. Another theory is that one can end up *"staying behind"* because of fear encountered at the

time of the death, resulting from not daring to move on towards, often described as the *'light at the end of a dark tunnel'*. This is believed by some to be the reason for the existence of child ghosts.

A *poltergeist*, a supernatural phenomenon believed to be responsible for making violent disturbances, such as throwing objects about, used to be thought of as a rogue spirit, but nowadays it is often viewed as a manifestation of a living person's hidden powers, which he or she doesn't know how to control.

The most recent surge of interest in paranormal phenomena was kick-started by reality television shows such as *The Ghost Hunters*, which aired from 2004 to 2016, where the viewers followed laypeople investigating reported hauntings. Social media, naturally, got involved, and nowadays there are a number of online sites where ordinary people can share their encounters with the likeminded. The premise is that anyone can be a ghost hunter with the aid of the electronic ghost detectors sold online.

Interest in ghosts has also given birth to a number of popular ghost tours, and even websites, where travellers can find British accommodation providers offering stays at their haunted inns and hotels.

Notably, the UK has one of the only academic research units in the world, that conducts studies in hauntings, near-death experiences, and dream precognitions. The University of Edinburgh's Koestler Parapsychology unit has been in operation since 1983, and is said to have proved that some people are able to receive telepathically sent messages from an individual sitting in another room.

Stories like this must make even the most sceptical ones amongst us, wonder what may lie beyond the world we perceive as real.

MAP OF DUNSTER

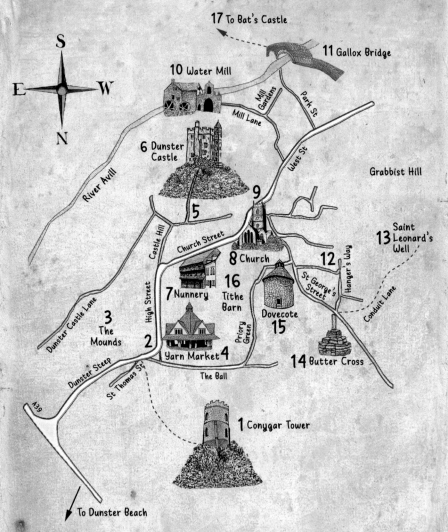

17 To Bat's Castle

11 Gallox Bridge

10 Water Mill

Mill Gardens

Mill Lane

Park St

West St

6 Dunster Castle

Grabbist Hill

River Avill

5

9

Saint
13 Leonard's
Well

Castle Hill

Church Street

8 Church

12

Hanger's Way

High Street

7 Nunnery

16 Tithe Barn

St George's Street

Conduit Lane

Dunster Castle Lane

3 The Mounds

2

Dovecote

15

Priory Green

Dunster Steep

St Thomas St

Yarn Market 4

The Ball

14 Butter Cross

A39

1 Conygar Tower

To Dunster Beach

1. Conygar Tower
2. The Luttrell Arms
3. The Mounds
4. Yarn Market
5. The Stables
6. Dunster Castle

7. The Nunnery
8. St George's Church & Graveyard
9. Spears Cross
10. Water Mill
11. Gallox Bridge

12. "New" Graveyard
13. St Leonard's Well
14. The Butter Cross
15. Dovecote
16. Tithe Barn
17. Bat's Castle

CHAPTER 3

AN EERIE WALKING GUIDE TO DUNSTER

Besides centuries old superstitions, folk tales and intriguing history, Dunster has a wealth of stories told of strange encounters with apparitions said to haunt its ancient streets and houses.

So, keep your eyes peeled and your heart rate steady while going on this walking tour around Dunster – just in case you run into the ghost cat, a little girl appearing in your hotel room at night, or the Roundhead haunting St George's churchyard. We wouldn't want you to become the next chapter in the long line of ghost stories told of Dunster.

DUNSTER'S CONYGAR HILL

Driving on the A39, the first thing that catches one's eye when approaching Dunster, besides the imposing castle, is the pretty Conygar tower perched high up on the hill, opposite Dunster Castle.

Many mistake it for a watchtower, but it is actually a folly, built in 1775 for purely decorative purposes by the owner of the castle at that time, Henry Fownes Luttrell. Henry wanted to see the tower from his castle, hence the three storey structure was built to be 18 metres high, and positioned on a hill, rising up on the north side of Dunster. The tower itself is empty inside, and can be accessed via a footpath starting from the bottom of St Thomas Street.

Even though the slopes and the bottom of the hill look quiet nowadays, this has not always been the case. On the village side, the same St Thomas Street, where the footpath departs from, was the beginning of the old route from Dunster to its harbour, located at the Lower Marsh.

In late medieval times, Dunster was a busy town with shops, tradesmen, and a market, which attracted people from all around the area, so the footfall in this part of Dunster would have been much larger than what it is nowadays.

Some historians believe that there may have been a medieval suburb, and a chapel, along St Thomas Street, previously known as *Rattle Row*. These possible buildings are long gone and the street nowadays houses mainly 19th and 20th century buildings.

An interesting detail is also that one of the fields on the slope of Conygar Hill, named *Butt Close* on an early map, may have been the site where Dunster men carried out their archery practice on Sunday mornings, as required by a law enacted in the 14th century to ensure England had enough men who knew how to use the longbow in times of war.

RABBITS' BREEDING GROUNDS

Rabbit meat was considered a luxury in Norman times and the Middle Ages, and it provided an important food supply for Dunster Castle and the townspeople. The story goes that the breeding of rabbits was eventually ceased on the hill, when the locals had had enough of the rabbits constantly escaping and destroying their precious vegetable gardens. The rabbits were eventually moved closer to Dunster beach, on the other side of the river from what is now Dunster Chalets' grounds, but the old name of the hill, '*coney*' meaning a rabbit and '*garth*' a garden or open space, stayed.

As can be expected, in a village with a history of buildings expanding over a thousand years, there is a wealth of stories relating to each part of the village, Conygar Hill area being no exception.

A MYSTERY TUNNEL

An interesting tale, still being told, talks of a mystery tunnel that was supposedly built to link Dunster Castle with Conygar Hill. A villager who the author spoke with, recalled that as a young boy only some 20-30 years ago, it was still common for the village children to hunt around the hill trying to find the entrance to the tunnel.

The origin of the tale is unknown, but the events that may have started it, can be traced back to the 17th century Civil War, when Dunster Castle was besieged by the Parliamentary troops. Desperate for the castle to surrender, General Blake brought in tunnellers and miners to try and undermine the massive curtain walls. This was to no avail, however, as when the mines were fired, only one caused damage. No evidence of the existence of this tunnel, however, has been found to this date.

BAD OMENS

When walking around Dunster's High Street it is hard not to notice the ominous looking flocks of black birds circling Conygar Hill. These are rooks, members of the Corvidae family, that have a long history of superstitions associated with them in Britain.

Rooks are traditionally accompanied by stories of bad fortune, especially if they arrive in an area in large flocks. They were believed to be able to sense the approach of death, and disaster, and have the ability to forecast the weather. There is also a belief claiming that if rooks were to abandon their rookery, the colonial nesting area, bad fortune, and even possible death, would fall onto the family who owned the land.

Such superstitions did not stop people from shooting these intelligent birds, however. During past centuries, rooks' meat was commonly eaten - by both the poor and the wealthy - with rook and rabbit pie being considered a delicacy by many.

Superstitions about birds still hold their ground in Britain. So much so, that there are some who do not like to bring any pictures, or statues of birds, into their homes.

The sound of loud caws definitely adds to the feel, and the eerie soundscape, of the village side of Conygar woods, which some – visitors and locals alike – find chilling.

SOUNDS OF MARCHING

One spooky story about Conygar Hill caught so much attention in the area, that it ended up being printed in the local newspaper in 1951. It tells of an incident witnessed by a group of tourists visiting Dunster, who wished to walk up Conygar Hill to see the tower.

While on the hill, they were all of a sudden disturbed by the sound of a large group of marching people approaching them. They looked around, but could not see anything. As the noise grew louder and louder, the group got so frightened that they all ran down the hill, only stopping when they reached the village. No explanation for the sounds was ever discovered.

Another, much more recent, but similar story tells of two separate visitors to Dunster Castle, who told the staff that, while standing on top of The Ball, the street right below Conygar Hill, they heard a distinct sound of people marching from The Ball down to the High Street. This same area is also the setting of another, first-hand story told to the author, of an apparition of a man seen walking from in front of the Luttrell Arms Hotel towards The Ball.

A sound of hooves has also been witnessed around this area at night. On one occasion, only a few years ago, a young man had his friends over for a party, and while standing outside chatting, they were stopped in their tracks by the clear sound of hooves. When they went to investigate, there were no horses to be found anywhere.

THE GREY MAN AND THE GHOST CAT

The present-day inhabitants of one particular house in this corner of Dunster village, have several stories to tell of the apparitions they have encountered in their house:

The husband: *"One day, about five years ago, I came back from work, and as I looked up I saw a person walking across the first floor landing. I called out to see if anybody was home, but no one answered. I remember distinctly the legs, covered in old men's dark trousers, and brown leather shoes."*

The wife: *"I do not know if that is the same apparition, but I have caught a glimpse of an old man with grey hair, and a wrinkly face walking around the house several times. I am not the only one who has seen him, a visitor to our house also saw the apparition. This grey man seems to appear more when there is some disturbance in the house, once I saw him walking through a partition wall we had made."*

"We also seemed to have a ghost cat in the house when we moved in. One night when we were relaxing on the sofa, watching television, a figure of a cat appeared from nowhere. We saw the apparition walking around the living room, and jumping off the tables, while we were watching over in amazement."

A MAN IN A TRICORN HAT

An even stranger story tells of an incident of a young man cutting the hedge at the bottom of Conygar Hill. All of a sudden he felt somebody go past him on the path. He stumbled slightly forward, looked up, but could not see anyone on the empty path. Feeling as if something invisible was near him, he took out his phone and took a photo. When he looked at his screen, he saw a picture of a man in a tricorn hat brandishing a sword.

THE HIGH STREET

O ne of the most photographed views of Dunster is the landscape that opens up from The Ball towards the High Street and Dunster Castle. It is easy to see why Dunster is frequently referred to as, not just one of the best preserved medieval villages in the UK, but also as one of the prettiest.

Though many of the facades have been altered over the centuries, the core structures of several houses on High Street date all the way back to the 14th and 15th centuries.

One of the oldest buildings on the High Street is located at 12–14 High Street, dendro-dated (a scientific method of dating tree rings to the exact year the tree was felled) to 1323. Another ancient building on the High Street, believed to date before 1305, is the middle part of what is nowadays the Luttrell Arms Hotel.

As is the case with most historic buildings, the houses on the High Street have had centuries of inhabitants making alterations according to the changing fashions of each era. The 17th century Civil War may also have been the cause of some of the changes. A surviving document mentions the sale of a piece of land at the bottom of Castle Hill, which specifies that there was a ruined house on the spot, on which the present-day house was built, after the Civil War, in the 1680s.

It is possible that many of the houses on the High Street were originally built as two-storey buildings, and the upper stories and facades were added later. For example, the three storey building at 30 High Street, which comprises of a retail space and living quarters, has a 19th century frontage, but, as discovered by the Historic England funded Early Dunster Project in 2020, hides behind it a structure dating back possibly as early as the 1600s. The same goes with the house built in 1323 located at 14 High Street of which the front was remodelled in the 1600s.

As the public cannot access private homes, a visit inside the businesses is highly recommended, as many of the spaces reveal interesting historic features.

MARKET TOWN

In the Middle Ages, following the construction of Dunster Castle, and the establishment of the Priory Church of St George, the little hamlet of Dunster grew into the most important town in the area, where, by the beginning of the 12th century, a weekly market was being held.

The location of the original market is not known, but documents mention that by the early 14th century the market was held on the High Street. A row of wooden market stalls, known as *'Shambles'* (an old English word meaning a place where meat is sold), ran down the centre of the street, and was still in place in the early 19th century.

An interesting feature of Dunster was also the number of inns. In 1687 there were as many as 22 persons licensed to sell alcohol in Dunster, but it's probable that some were simply for licences to sell home-brewed ale on market days.

YARN MARKET

One of Dunster's best known landmarks, the Yarn Market, is also located on the High Street. It was built around 1609 by George Luttrell, heir to the Dunster estates, to provide a cover for the market sellers. Though Dunster's market declined during the 18th century, it remained an important local centre, and was more or less self-sufficient up until the middle of the 20th century, with joiners, tailors, hatters, bakers, butchers, blacksmiths and wheelwrights offering their services.

STONE CROSSES

In medieval times it was customary for many English towns to have crosses standing in the market places. These crosses, besides reminding the passers-by of Christian teachings, acted as local landmarks.

Dunster's High Street also used to have two stone crosses. It is believed that one of Dunster's crosses, the *High Cross,* was located where the Yarn Market is now. The other, the *Butter Cross*, so named as it was the place where dairy products were sold, is believed to have been located on the south end of the High Street.

The BUTTER CROSS, which was moved to its present location on the side of St George's Street in the late 18th century, is nowadays missing the upper part of the shaft and the cross arms. How or when the Butter Cross was damaged is not recorded, but there are speculations that this may have happened during the 17th century Civil War, or during the religious upheaval of the 16th century English Reformation, when some people started regarding such crosses as superstitious.

STORIES FROM THE HIGH STREET

As expected, Dunster's High Street, with so many old houses still intact, is home to many odd tales.

LOVELY SCENTS LINGERING IN THE AIR

One of the ladies in the village told the author a story of the time when she was expecting a child, and quite often, feeling poorly. Every time there was a complication, she would have a sensation of a beautiful scent lingering inside the house. She said it reminded her of an old soap smell. The scent got stronger and stronger as the pregnancy proceeded. This lady had had prior experience with otherworldly phenomena, so when the scent got so strong she could not take it anymore, she spoke out loud and asked for the smells to stop. After that, she says, the scents never returned inside the house.

The same lady told the author of the beautiful, fresh linen scent she and her child would smell in their back garden, years later. The scent would be detectable in the place where, in the old days, there used to be a tailor's workspace, and where he would have kept his fabrics. The lady said that she has never felt afraid in her house. *"The scents were always lovely. The tailor must have been very happy, while he lived in this house that we now own".*

A BED FULL OF COINS

One of the owners of a High Street house told the author that odd things happen regularly in their building. One night in the 2010s the owner woke up in the middle of the night, threw the blankets off and shouted in panic to his wife: *"Take the blankets off, take the blankets off, there is money all over the bed."* The next morning the wife told the relatives staying with them about the bad night's sleep she had had. Before she had a chance to elaborate on what had happened, she was told that when their guest had gone to the toilet during the night, she had been met by the sight of an apparition of a man with a long white hair and beard, sitting by their kitchen table, on a high backed old chair, counting money.

A LADY IN THE HALLWAY

A woman living on the High Street told a story about her young daughter, who constantly talked about a lady she kept on seeing in their hallway. The girl would bid good night to the lady every night. She also kept on talking about a man in their front room wearing a big hat and a wonky smile. She was never afraid of the apparitions - on the contrary, she was seen on several occasions laughing heartily, while looking at the corner of the front room, where the parents saw nothing but empty space.

PSYCHIC DOGS

Many people in Britain believe that animals are more sensitive than humans in detecting supernatural phenomena. There are stories of at least two local ladies whose dogs refuse to go into three of the buildings located on the High Street, and one on West Street. When one of these dogs was forced into one of these commercial buildings, the owner said that her dog would walk oddly sideways, and constantly tried to get out, as if paralysed with fear.

SOMETIMES THERE IS A RATIONAL EXPLANATION

Sometimes there is a rational explanation for a strange phenomenon. The present-day owner of one of the hotels on the High Street, told the author that his staff were adamant that there was a ghost on the premises. They told the owner that the service bell kept on ringing by itself when no one was near it. The owner, not a great believer in ghosts, investigated and realised that when a staff member walked past the bell, he would sometimes set the bell swinging slightly, and some ten seconds later the clapper would touch the side of the bell, making the bell sound.

A PHANTOM CUSTOMER

There is also a recent story of a phantom customer coming into one of the shops on the High Street. The female staff member of that time had been arranging the shelves when she heard the door open, and shut behind her. When she turned around to welcome the customer, she saw an apparition of a woman by the door. While she was watching the apparition in disbelief, the figure of the woman walked through the shop, and through the back wall in the spot where there used to be a door leading to the main part of the building. As expected, the shop assistant was quite puzzled by the experience.

Another story about the same building talks of its past inhabitants witnessing an apparition of a man walking down the stairs inside the living quarters of the house. This apparition is said to have been encountered several times by the owners of the building, and the story caused much wonder in the village.

WOULD THE STAFF COME TO WORK IF THEY KNEW?

When asked to share stories, some of the business owners were worried that if the staff knew about the incidents, they might be too scared to come to work. The staff that the author spoke with, however, actually seemed to enjoy reliving the thrill of the odd encounters, and the stories they had been told.

One story, shared with the author, recalled incidents told by a chef who used to work in one of the High Street establishments. The chef had, on numerous occasions, told his fellow staff members of tins and utensils, which kept on moving around on the shelves. Another, similar story told of another business on the same street, describes odd incidents where boxes would fall down without any rational explanation, and products left at certain places after closing time, would be found the following morning somewhere else.

One female staff member working at the same business where the odd kitchen incidents occurred, also told her fellow workers that she had encountered an apparition of a round faced, kind looking woman with curly hair, while cleaning the premises at the end of the day. Her fellow workers believed the figure she had seen might have been the *"lovely woman"* who used to own the business some decades earlier.

AN ENTITY BY THE WINDOW

It is not just the staff members, or the owners of the buildings, though, who have had odd encounters on Dunster's High Street. There are several stories of customers walking into business premises and right away, quite boldly, voicing out what they were sensing in the building. One business owner said she had a female customer walk through the doors, who immediately said that she felt an entity sitting by the shop window. The owner didn't quite know how to respond to the information, but, fortunately, was not too startled.

SOMEONE IN THE BEDROOM

There is also a story doing rounds in the village, of a woman who was renting one of the houses at the south end of the High Street. The story goes that she woke up in the middle of the night, when she distinctly felt somebody sitting down on her bed. She thought it was her boyfriend, but quickly realised he wasn't in the house at the time.

Another story tells of a girl living on the High Street, who was adamant for years that there was an old woman sitting in her bedroom. The mother believed it may have been the grandmother of the family who used to own the house. The same girl would see an apparition of two children wandering around her mother's house. The apparitions did not feel malevolent in anyway, and the family lived happily in the house for many years.

BABY CRYING

Another woman and her adult daughter told the author of their slightly more eerie experiences in the house which they used to own on the High Street.

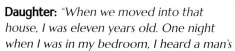

Mother: *"That was the first house ever, where I could feel spirits. One night when I was in bed by myself, I heard somebody walk across my bedroom. The sound of the steps stopped, and then carried on, straight out of the room. I didn't see anything, just heard the very clear footsteps."*

Daughter: *"When we moved into that house, I was eleven years old. One night when I was in my bedroom, I heard a man's voice, right outside my door, call my name twice. I thought it was my father, and shouted, 'Hold on, I'm coming'. When I opened the door, there was no one there. Both my father and my brother were at the other end of the house, and had not been anywhere near my bedroom door."*

Daughter: *"Another time, when I was sitting in one of the rooms by myself, in the winter time, with all the windows and doors shut, the solid, heavy Georgian door swung all the way open, without anyone touching it."*

The time when the family felt rather spooked out, was when they started hearing the sounds of a baby crying, coming from one of the top floor rooms.

Mother: *"It was an absolutely beautiful room with exposed beams, but the crying, which we all heard several times, did scare our young daughter."*

"I am normally a right scaredy cat myself, but, incredibly, I was never afraid in that house. The house really pulled you in, so much so that it was hard to leave when we finally sold it. You could feel the emotions of the people who had lived there in the past. If I had told my parents, that I was contemplating on using an exorcist, my parents would have thought that I had lost my mind. I come from a background, where I would have never entertained the idea of ghosts being real. Not until I moved into that house."

THE LUTTRELL ARMS, THE MOUNDS & THE CIVIL WAR IN DUNSTER

THE LUTTRELL ARMS

The Grade II* listed building that nowadays houses The Luttrell Arms Hotel and restaurant, consists of three ancient houses, the middle of which being the oldest, dating possibly to the end of the 13th century or the beginning of the 14th century. One of the grandest buildings in the present-day village, it is believed to have originated as a large courtyard house built for a high-ranking person.

The building, which was heavily altered in the 1600s and turned into an inn in the middle of the same century, is a must-see for lovers of history, architecture and interior design. It houses numerous beautiful features such as the two-storey gabled stone entrance porch, the bar area's magnificent carved oak window, a large open fireplace, and the heavy moulded oak ceiling beams.

The back garden offers great views to the Dunster Castle, where you can also find a gate leading onto the Dunster Castle grounds, and to the mounds, where one of the episodes of the Civil War, was fought.

CIVIL WAR IN DUNSTER

The English Civil War (1642-1651), was fought between the Parliamentarians (or 'Roundheads', so called as some wore their hair cropped round the head, in contrast to the courtly fashion of long ringlets), and the Royalists ('Cavaliers'). The series of what were at first mainly local conflicts were fought over differences of opinions relating to religious freedom, and how England should be governed. The war and its aftermath was a massive upheaval, not only for the Dunsterians, but also for all the people living in the British Isles, with an estimated 200,000 people losing their lives.

At the outbreak of the conflict, the then owner of Dunster Castle, Thomas Luttrell, declared for Parliament, and held off two Royalist attacks in 1642 and 1643, the latter led by Colonel Frances Wyndham, who owned a large estate in nearby Williton. After the 1643 attack Thomas was persuaded to switch to the Royalist side, and when he died in 1644, Colonel Wyndham, the cousin of Thomas Luttrell's wife, was declared governor of Dunster Castle.

In the autumn of 1645, the Bridgwater based Parliamentarian Colonel Robert Blake and his 600 men arrived in Dunster with orders to seize the castle. Blake and his officers moved in to the Luttrell Arms, at that time known as the *Ship Inn*, and stationed their troops around the castle - across the lawns, at Gallox Bridge, Loxhole Bridge, Frackford, May Hill and the lower slopes of Grabbist Hill. Blake also placed field artillery on the ridge behind the Luttrell Arms - a ridge, which is believed to have been possibly raised up to its present level during the siege to place the Parliamentarian cannons on, and to shelter the soldiers from the returning fire from the castle. The ridge may have been raised to shelter the soldiers, but there is also another, persistent though unverified local story claiming that the ridge hides beneath it a mass grave for the soldiers who died during the siege.

Despite weeks of bombardment the Parliamentary cannons could not penetrate Dunster Castle's massive curtain wall, and so Blake brought in miners to try and undermine the wall. Only one mine did damage, and in such disadvantaged spot that Blake decided not to attack.

By the spring of 1646 Blake's army surrounding Dunster Castle totalled around 2,000 men and Wyndham agreed to negotiate a surrender. In April 1646 Wyndham and his troops were allowed to march out of the castle. Three years later King Charles I was executed, and in 1651 the English Civil War ended with victory to the Parliamentarians.

Unfortunately very few hard facts exist from which to gain a definite understanding of the consequences of the siege for the people living in Dunster. The burial records

for Dunster in this period have not survived, but there is a record stating that as many as forty houses were burnt down during the siege.

One interesting story concerning the Civil War in Dunster is that of the hole in one of the timbers in the roof of the Yarn Market, located right in front of the Luttrell Arms. This hole was allegedly made by a cannon ball, fired from Dunster Castle during the siege. Some doubt the story due to the improbable trajectory route of a cannon ball hitting the spot where the timber is located today. However, it is possible that the timber is not in its original place, as the Yarn Market was rebuilt in 1647 owing to the damage caused by the fighting in Dunster.

STORIES

Even though the Luttrell Arms is a real haven for visitors who love history, this building is also home to many fascinating stories for those who enjoy otherworldly tales.

A SENSITIVE DACHSHUND

An interesting story, told to the author by a female villager, recounts odd incidents involving her three beloved dachshunds.

"Around 13 years ago, before we moved to Dunster, my husband and I were staying at The Luttrell Arms with our long-haired dachshund called Dougal. He was a lovely, calm dog, and therefore we were surprised to notice how he became restless inside what is nowadays called the guest lounge. He kept on barking at the left hand side of the fireplace, even though we didn't see anything there. When the barking and whining got worse, we retired to our room with me carrying him over my shoulder as he was so upset. Usually, when we stayed at a hotel, he would sleep happily in his travel cage, but that night he was up all night looking at the bedroom door, whining."

"In the morning, I took him out for a walk through the back of the Luttrell Arms, and his odd behaviour continued. He was barking around the trees, even though there was nothing there to be seen. We had talked with the staff about Dougal's strange behaviour, and when we returned to the hotel, the manager asked what Dougal had been barking at. The manager then said that other guests had reported seeing an apparition of an old lady standing on the left hand side of the fireplace in the guest lounge, right where Dougal was barking at, and also at the door of the bedroom we stayed in."

A GHOST DOG

There are also other stories involving dogs at the Luttrell Arms. Dunster is renowned for being a dog friendly village, and apparently so much so that some dogs never want to leave. The stories talk of guests sitting down in the bar area, when they have suddenly felt a sensation of a dog rubbing against their legs. Expecting to find another guest's dog next to their chair, and leaning over to give it a stroke, they are said to have been baffled to find nothing there.

A MONK BEHIND THE BAR

Another tale told of the Luttrell Arms bar area is that of an apparition of a monk seen behind the counter. This monk, the story goes, has been seen by several members of the staff and visitors.

Interestingly, some historians have linked the Luttrell Arms Hotel to Cleeve Abbey believing that the original building may have been built for, or at least later housed the abbot of the nearby abbey, making it possible that in the past there were monks visiting, and living, in the building.

RECEPTIONIST

There is also a story of a receptionist who used to work in the hotel in the 1980s. During night shifts she would be alone in the reception, located next to the bar area, and told her husband that she had more than once had a guest come down in the middle of the night from one particular room asking if they could change their room as they had encountered an apparition of a woman.

A DOOR OPENING BY ITSELF

Another story from the reception area tells of a local woman who was helping out at the hotel reception during one Christmas period. While she was standing at the reception, she was amazed to see the large, heavy door next to the reception open several times by itself. She said it was impossible that a door of that weight could open by itself due to a draught.

AN APPARITION OF A YOUNG GIRL

There are also several stories of sightings of an apparition of a young girl walking around the Luttrell Arms Hotel, and even having a conversation with a daughter of one of the guests inside their bedroom. The daughter had not been scared, but had said to the receptionist when the family was checking out the next morning, that for the next visit, she would perhaps prefer to stay in another room.

A CLEANER'S WORK IS NEVER FINISHED

There is a recent story of a housekeeper working at the hotel, who told the author that while she and another cleaner had been tidying up one of the guest rooms, she had encountered a strange incident. She said that she had finished making up the bed, straightening every crease of the duvet cover, and then turned away for a few seconds. When she cast her eyes back on the bed there was a clear impression on the bed, as if somebody had sat on it. The former cleaner, when recounting the story, was still, years after, visibly shaken by the incident.

A PHOTO OF A WOMAN IN THE WINDOW

An interesting piece of 20th century history can also be found at the Luttrell Arms' entrance corridor. Two framed photographs on the wall, captured by a guest in the first half of the 1900s, show a tall woman standing by a second floor window, looking out onto the street. The photographer is said to have claimed that when he took the photo, all the windows of the hotel were devoid of people. Whether true or a hoax, this photograph ties in with the fashionable interest in spirit photography in Britain, which started at the beginning of the 19th century, and continued well into the 20th century.

CHURCH STREET

Nowadays Church Street is the main road joining High Street to West Street. Here you will find a selection of charming old cottages, and retail spaces on both sides of the narrow thoroughfare, the 15th century Nunnery, the Village Gardens, the Grade I listed St George's Church and the medieval church house facing the old churchyard, recognised by its dark timber cladding added in the 1800s.

Some 15th century documents refer to this oddly shaped street as *New Street*, and it may be that the original main thoroughfare may have actually gone up Castle Steep, and continued down to West Street. This road is still in use nowadays, but mainly as an access for Dunster Castle and to the houses located on both sides of this pretty road.

The impressive three storey building called the NUNNERY (even though there is no evidence of any nuns having ever lived there) is one of the many interesting buildings in the village. A deed dated 1346 refers to a grant of land in Dunster to Cleeve Abbey, and it has been assumed that this is when the Nunnery was built. Recent dendro-dating of the roof timbers, however, gives a 15th century build-date. The original purpose of the building is unclear, but some historians believe there may have been shops on the ground floor, and lodgings above.

The present-day name of the building, *The Nunnery*, dates back to 1760 - before that it was called the *High House*. The name may have come about from an early document which refers to Cleeve Abbey as a *'convent'*, which originally meant any sort of religious house for both sexes, not just one for women.

The entrance to the VILLAGE GARDENS, maintained by village volunteers, is located just a stone's throw away from the Nunnery, and is accessed from Church Street through a wrought iron gate in the garden's high stone wall. It is open all year around for both visitors and locals, and makes a wonderfully tranquil spot to relax in, while having a break from sightseeing. You can also walk through the village gardens to reach the other locations of the odd encounters mentioned in this book, the Tithe Barn, the Dovecote and the Priory Green.

STORIES

1964 NEWSPAPER ARTICLE

In the 1960s, while the Nunnery was a guest house, an incident that happened in the building appeared in the local newspapers. The article stated that a woman staying at the guest house, woke up in the middle of the night and saw a figure of a woman, wearing white, flowing robes, standing at the bottom of her bed. When the startled guest screamed, the figure disappeared. The noise woke her husband up, who did not see the apparition. The article does not mention whether or not the couple packed their bags and left, or if they dared to stay another night in the building.

THE TOP FLOOR ROOM

An owner of one of the houses on Church Street told the author of an incident which took place only a few years ago, while the owner was having renovations done by a father and a son team. The son was working by himself on the top floor room, when he felt someone standing behind him. He thought it was his father, and before he had a chance to turn around, he heard a voice, which wasn't his father's, saying: *"What do you think you are doing?"* He quickly turned around, only to realise that he was alone in the room, and that there was no one behind him. After that the son refused to continue working in that room.

KNOCKING

There are many accounts from around the world, and throughout different eras, of possessed objects; i.e. items to which spirits are believed to have become attached. The objects in the stories vary from mirrors, paintings and jewellery to dolls, clothing and furniture. Possibly the best known stories relate to the Kohinoor and Hope diamonds, the Screaming Skull and the Annabelle doll.

Dunster, also, has at least two stories of such objects. One talks about a piano playing by itself in Dunster Castle, and the other of an old wardrobe located inside one of the houses on Church Street.

This Church Street house was owned by a medium at the time, who, while in the room where this wardrobe was located, all of a sudden heard a loud knocking coming from inside the wardrobe. She opened the wardrobe doors, but there was no one inside, and nothing visible that could have caused such a clear, knocking sound. The story does not tell if the medium tried to free the old wardrobe of the spirit believed to be trapped in it, or not, before her own passing on. The wardrobe is still in its place, but the present-day owner, a relative of the medium, has not encountered anything out of the ordinary.

A BALL OF LIGHT FLYING THROUGH THE HOUSE

There is a story of another old house in Church Street where the mother of the family living in it at the time, witnessed a ball of light flying through the house. She could not explain what it was, but was quite fascinated by the event, when she recounted the story to the author.

She also said that when a team of historians came to inspect her house, as part of an archaeological project being done in the village, they found a mummified cat under the stairs. The owner said that she wasn't overly happy about the team removing the cat from where it was buried at, as she knew that the removal was considered as bad luck.

A GUARDIAN SPIRIT

A very different, but equally intriguing story was told to the author by a woman who recently moved to the village:

"When I moved into my house in 2022, it was winter, and the central heating did not work. I would light the fire in the old fireplace downstairs and sleep in the room to keep warm. I didn't sleep very well there at all, and one night, when I was finally fast asleep, I woke up at 3 am to the sound of voices. I got up and realised that the radio, which I had left for the builders to listen to while working, was on. I thought that someone must have not switched it off properly."

"The following night, I was woken up around 3 am again, to the radio turning itself on. Now, this time I knew that it had been turned off, as I had checked it before going to sleep. When I woke up, I realised that the room was full of smoke from the fire."

"I feel that someone was looking over me, and waking me up, as I could have otherwise died of carbon monoxide poisoning. Perhaps it was a past resident that I could not see, someone being kind. In the one and a half years that I have lived in the house now, I have never felt any fear. The chimney-sweep, however, made me buy a carbon monoxide monitor from an online shop, before he agreed to leave the house. He also made me promise never to sleep in that room again when the fire was on."

DUNSTER'S BENEDICTINE PRIORY

A small Benedictine monastery was established in Dunster in the 12th century. The priory was located on the north side of the present-day St George's church, but unfortunately most of the buildings have been lost over the centuries.

When the British archaeological Time Team, conducted their *'Dig Village'* project in Dunster between 2013 and 2018, they found the base of ancient walls behind St George's Church. It is believed that these walls may have been part of the foundations of the Benedictine Priory's dormitory and refectory building. They also found evidence of a doorway on the first floor of the church tower, evolving into a theory that at some point there may have been a corridor between the dormitory and the church, making it easier for the monks to reach the church at night, without having to venture outdoors.

The only remaining part of the priory is the building attached to St George's Church, nowadays called The Old Priory. This building has been dendro dated to 1286, making it one of the oldest still intact in Dunster. The assumption is that this building was the Prior's Hall of the Benedictine priory.

Dunster's 16th century dovecote

It is believed that during the 300-400 years of its existence, the priory also had its own vineyard and a farm, cultivated by the monks to provide them with vegetables, fruits and herbs.

After the dissolution of the monasteries in 1536 the Priory area continued to be used as a farm by the new land owners, and some of the buildings that remain - such as the 16th century Tithe Barn and DOVECOTE date from that time.

The priory also had its own well, located on the northeast side of Grabbist Hill. The water from this ST LEONARD'S WELL was taken to a wellhead located in Conduit Lane, and from there to the priory and two public troughs, one located in St George's churchyard, and the other on what is now the High Street. The well house covering the well dates back to the 16th century, and can be reached by a 15 minute walk on the track leading left near the top of St George's Street. This well is reputed in some texts to have curative powers for eye problems.

STORIES

Amongst the most famous ghost stories circulating around Dunster village, are those of the numerous sightings of monks seen walking on the Priory Green, and in the little square between the Memorial Garden, the Tithe Barn and the Dovecote.

One of the stories talks of an apparition of a monk bearing two pails of milk suspended from a yoke, crossing the Priory Green road, in front of two local ladies, who, since then, the story goes, have not been too happy to walk on the road by themselves.

Another story talks of a group of children walking on the Priory Green road to Dunster School one morning, when one of the boys stopped suddenly, and with a terrified face, pointed at something, that was not visible to the other children.

A friend of a villager, visiting from London, and described by the villager telling the story to the author, as a respectable and trustworthy person, also swore that he saw a monk walk towards him on the Priory Green in broad daylight. The visitor, unaware of the stories circulating in the village, described the apparition as being so vivid, that the man first took the monk to be a real person.

ST GEORGE'S CHURCH

The Grade I listed, Priory Church of St George is one of the most magnificent buildings in Dunster. The exact year of the original construction is not known, but the work is believed to have begun around the end of the 11th century by the order of William de Mohun, the first Lord of Dunster. The church, the majority of which dates from the 1400s, is built in a cruciform shape with a 15th century tower looming over it, surrounded by a churchyard and graves.

The churchyard, possibly as old as the church, is believed by some to be the final resting place of tens of thousands of people, and was regularly used for burials until the new churchyard, accessed from St George's Street, was opened in the 1800s.

The much admired, 15th century carved oak rood screen inside the church, believed to be the longest in Britain, was built after a dispute over the use of the church flared up between the Dunster Priory monks, and the parishioners. The result of the dispute was that the church was divided into two. The east chancel was used by the Dunster Priory monks, and the west side by the parishioners.

Nowadays laymen are allowed to wander freely on both sides of the screen and admire the paintings, stained glass windows, and the masterly carved woodwork.

The church, and the private graveyard on the east side of the church, contain the tombs of the Luttrell family, who owned Dunster Castle, and the lands around it, for 600 years. The vast space and lack of hordes of tourists make visiting this church a calming experience, if you are not spooked by the stories of the churchyard, which many believe to be haunted.

The fear of evil spirits permeated all layers of society during the Middle Ages. Just as with many other grand churches and cathedrals, Dunster's St George's Church builders, and later renovators, decorated the walls, not just with saints and religious symbols, but with GROTESQUES, and gargoyles to ward off evil spirits.

While some of the fierce stone icons served a functional purpose - like the gargoyles draining water from the roof of St George's south entrance - most of the grotesques found at St George's are decorative. The fear-evoking faces, such as the ones adorning the west entrance, with their empty eyes and fangs, are believed by some historians to have functioned in medieval English society as reminders of the monsters that may await in the afterlife, if the parishioners chose not to lead a good Christian life.

In medieval times the north side of the churchyard was also associated with evil, with the north door often known as the DEVIL'S DOOR. In many British churches it was common practice to leave the north door ajar to let evil spirits out, especially during baptisms. Churches were also commonly built on the north side of roads, to enable the main entrance to be facing south, as is the case with Dunster's St George's Church.

STONE POWDER carved out of interior, and exterior, surfaces of British churches and effigies like those found inside St George's Church, was believed to hold curative powers in the Middle Ages. The dust was gathered by common people, as well as healers and cunning folk, applied to water or wine, and drank as a cure-all for various illnesses. The folk belief of the power of rocks, however, stems back beyond the Middle Ages, and England. The Ancient Sumerians, Egyptians, and Greeks are believed to have also used stones for protection, and for curative purposes.

YEW TREES, like the the ancient yew in St George's churchyard, the remaining fragments of which is believed to be derived from the original main trunk, were also believed to drive away evil spirits. Perhaps for this reason, yew trees are found in churchyards all over Britain, some believed to be dating back to pre-Christian pagan sites of worship, making them older than the churchyards they stand on.

The beliefs surrounding the sacred yew can be found not just in England, but in other countries as well. European and English druids are believed to have revered the yew as sacred, as did the ancient Greeks, who associated yew with the goddess of death, *Hecate*.

In the Middle Ages, a CHURCH GRIM was believed to be the guardian spirit whose function was to protect the churchyard from evil people and spirits. In some parts of Britain when a new churchyard was opened, it was believed that the first person buried had to guard the churchyard from all kinds of evil. To prevent such a burden from falling on a human soul, a black dog was sometimes buried in the north part of the churchyard, hence making the church yard encounters with black dogs, and other church grims, common features in medieval English folktales.

St George's churchyard in Dunster is also the home of many ghost stories. Amongst the best-known ones are stories of encounters with ROUNDHEADS that wander, not just in the churchyard, but around the village and Dunster Castle.

One recent story talks of a couple, who, while visiting Dunster, passed through St George's churchyard. In broad daylight, they all of a sudden encountered an apparition of a man dressed in full Roundhead uniform walking towards them. The apparition was not just visual, but, the story goes, addressed the woman by her name, asking, *'Are you coming home Jane?'*, and then walked away. The husband saw and heard the apparition speak as well, and described it as incredibly vivid. When the startled couple escaped to the inside of the church, where a local event was taking place at the time, the couple asked the villagers if the church was haunted, and told them what had just happened in the churchyard.

Another story talks of the STRANGE LIGHTS regularly seen in St George's churchyard. A woman, who used to live in St George's Street, and whose house abutted the churchyard, told the other villagers, that she would frequently see bright ORBS flying about the churchyard, when she looked out of the back window of her house.

One recent first-hand account of an incident which took place in the churchyard is certainly amongst the eeriest told of Dunster. A man described to the author how he, while walking his dog just before midnight on Priory Green, passed St George's Lych gate, and saw a figure that he thought was a woman dressed in a long black cape standing on the church path. The man greeted her, as is customary in Dunster, but as the figure turned around to face the man, the apparition produced massive wings and took off over the yew tree before disappearing. The man was stunned with fear, and badly shaken when he returned home to recount his story.

No wonder then that some people remark that they find the old churchyard rather eerie, and prefer not to walk through it by themselves at night.

WEST STREET

West Street, surrounded by colourful cottages, is nowadays the main thoroughfare from Dunster village to Exmoor. Some of the oldest houses, which to this day continue to be inhabited, date back to the 1300s, and were built using a medieval *'true cruck'* structure, a naturally curved timber to support the roofs. This is a structure that is found nowadays only in the very oldest surviving English houses.

At the top end of West Street, at the junction of Church Street and St George's Street, lies the Spear's Cross, which is believed to be the core of the earliest, possibly Anglo-Saxon settlement in the village, and named such due to a cross that used to be located there.

The exact location of the 15 households that the Domesday book of 1086 mentions is not known, but if the hypothesis that Spears Cross was the original site of Dunster's market, is true, it is possible that the houses mentioned in the Domesday book may have been located in the old Spears Cross area.

Even though many of the village's businesses nowadays can be found on the High Street, this has not always been the case. West Street buildings have housed a great number of businesses over the centuries, including butchers, bakers, grocers, drapers, dressmakers, carpenters, boot makers and painters. The village hospital was located here, as was the pound, and the alms house, which was turned into a Victorian work house in 1839. There is a record of West Street also having stables, from where locals and travellers could hire horses.

One of the newer buildings on West Street, well worth a visit, even just to admire its pretty exterior, is the Old Methodist Chapel, built in 1878, and turned into business premises at the end of the 20th century.

PLAGUE IN DUNSTER

A frequently recounted tale of West Street is that of the supposed plague doors that were believed to have been cut into the existing walls between the cottages. The story goes that during the plague outbreaks in Dunster, the house owners would use the doors to move around West Street, thus avoiding having to go outdoors, and to breathe in what was believed to be, poisonous air. The story, however, has not been verified, and it is believed by some that it originated from a 19th century tale told by one of the Dunster's alehouse owners.

What is a fact, however, is that there are written records of a plague hitting Dunster hard in 1645. The records tell us that in May 1645, the fifteen-year-old Prince Charles was sent from Bristol to Dunster owing to a bad outbreak of the plague in Bristol. What the court and the prince's father, King Charles I, did not know was that by then, the plague was also rampant in Dunster.

The prince stayed at Dunster Castle for just two weeks, mostly confined to his bedroom, where he is said to have felt deeply uneasy. The story tells that the young prince's uneasiness was not so much due to a fear of the plague, but because of the eerie feeling he had in the room, which constantly disturbed his sleep. After two weeks, the young prince, later to become King Charles II, was moved to Barnstaple for safety.

It is impossible to say how many people actually died in Dunster due to the plague, but the surviving records show that in May 1645 alone, 24 people were buried in Dunster. This was a massive increase to the average of 30 deaths per year recorded during the previous five years.

The trail also goes cold after May 1645, and the next time the parish holds death and marriage records, is from 1660. This may be owing to records being lost, the vicar dying of plague, or that owing to the lack of clergy, there were not enough literate people around to keep the registers up-to-date. Through the outbreaks that plagued Britain for hundreds of years, a shortage of clergy was a definite problem, as many died tending the sick.

No records of Dunster remain from 1348, the year the plague first entered Britain, thus making it impossible to know how Dunster fared through the first outbreak. The bacteria arrived in Weymouth onboard a ship from Europe, and according to recorded history, quickly spread across the South-West and Bristol. The disease was caused by a plague bacterium, *Yersinia pestis*, first carried by rodent fleas and infected humans, and later becoming airborne. The first wave of 1348-49 is said to have killed 30-50 percent of the entire English population. In 1361-62 the plague returned to England, this time killing around one fifth of the remaining population.

It is believed that Dunster may also have been hit by plague more than once. The records show that there was a great surge of deaths in 1596, believed by some historians to fit into the scenario of a deadly, fast spreading, and basically incurable disease like the plague, going on a rampage in Dunster.

The poor levels of hygiene were partly to blame for the quick spread of the disease in England and in Europe. In 14th century England people lived in tight quarters with filth everywhere. There was no running water, and streets were basically open sewers, with garbage and animal carcasses thrown into ditches and rivers. The floors of homes and inns were covered in grasses with only the top level being replaced and the bottom left untouched, sometimes for years. Fleas, rats and diseases flourished. Medical knowledge was hardly existent with odd cures such as bleeding and induced vomiting being prescribed by doctors.

During the period when many of the houses on West Street were being built, the plague hit Somerset several times, in some cases wiping out whole communities and generations of families within weeks. The population had no immunity to the bacteria, and when the disease developed into a pneumonic plague, and became airborne, spreading from person to person via cough droplets, the fatality of the infected was nearly 100 percent.

The speed with which the disease travelled must have made the epidemic even more terrifying in Dunster. When a completely healthy person could die within days of showing the first symptoms, covered in boils and blackened skin, how could anyone be safe?

No wonder then that people tried everything within their power to protect themselves and their loved ones. As the cause of the disease was unknown, superstitions were rampant. The plague was widely seen as a punishment from God for sins, with many preachers blaming witchcraft, and a lack of piety. Physicians

prescribed tobacco, brimstone smoke, and herbs as prevention, the quack doctors chicken feathers, and powdered unicorn horn.

Many of the clergy continued to tend to the sick, with some sources claiming that owing to this, Somerset lost nearly half of its clergy during the first outbreak.

With massive mortality rates and the lack of work force, the social balance of society started shifting from the 14th century onwards. The working class and the tenant farmers, many of whom were tied to the land they worked on, were not allowed to leave their area without the permission of the landlord, and subsequently became more vocal owing to the skills of the surviving tradesmen becoming more sought after. Many working class people also inherited - in some cases, several of their deceased relatives' possessions.

Plague is also said to have changed the attitudes of people as it killed people from all different classes: if the nobility could catch this mysterious illness, were they really any better than the rest of society? Common men began to doubt the power of the nobility and the clergy, a notion which had gone unquestioned for centuries.

SPOOKY STORIES FROM WEST STREET

VICTORIAN DRUMMER BOY

Besides the story of the plague doors between West Street houses, there are plenty of more recent odd tales told of the houses on this street. One of these stories talks of a medium who used to live on West Street and who told the villagers of the ongoing encounters she had had with a young Victorian drummer boy in her house. The apparition, dressed in a uniform and a little hat, the story goes, kept on following the owner around the house, sometimes even sitting next to her on the sofa, when she was watching television in the evenings. The medium was said to have had a gift for helping spirits move on, but the story doesn't tell if she managed to help this poor little drummer boy, or if he still haunts the house.

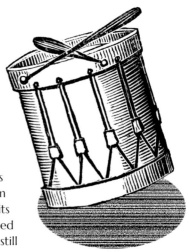

ROMAN SOLDIERS

Another story told to the author talks of a couple who had bought one of these beautiful, centuries old houses on West Street. One night, while lying in bed, the couple all of a sudden witnessed a silhouette of what appeared to be Roman soldiers, in full dress and helmets, marching out of their bedroom wall, right next to their bed. While the couple looked on in total disbelief, the men marched out through the opposing wall and disappeared. The couple told villagers the next morning that they could not believe how they both could see the soldiers in such detail. The couple also recounted that the whole time they lived in the property they had never felt alone.

Since then interestingly, the *Time Team* has found a number of Roman pottery remains in Dunster village, and on Dunster beach. This has resulted in some researchers suspecting that there may have been a Roman settlement in Dunster and that the port was not founded in the Middle Ages, as was believed to be the case before, but may actually date back to Roman times.

RESIDENT GHOST

When the author was collecting stories for this book, one house in particular on West Street kept on cropping up in the stories told by the past and present-day villagers. The stories talk of a rocking chair moving by itself, boxes found thrown around a storeroom, a glass moving and dropping off an even shelf without anyone touching it, a figure appearing behind a guest's back while inside the building, and the outside door opening and closing by itself. Some of these stories have also been shared on various online sites that focus on paranormal activities in Britain.

A WOMAN BAKING BREAD

One of the Dunster ladies living on West Street told the author of a strange incident that happened in her house some years ago. A friend of hers, while visiting her house, saw an apparition of an elderly lady baking bread in her kitchen. The apparition was not malevolent or frightening, but quite on the contrary, she said, the lady seemed very nice and friendly. The same owner said that she feels that her house is very peaceful, but she does hear sighing occasionally, always coinciding with the death of someone she knows.

DUNSTER GALLOWS

A t the bottom end of West Street, turning left towards the old packhorse bridge lies one of the main ancient routes to Dunster. The road, nowadays called Park Street, used to be divided into two, the bottom end being called *Gallox Street*, and the top end, *Water Street*. The early settlement of fifteen households mentioned in the Domesday book of 1086, if not located around the Spears Cross area, most likely would have been found here.

The packhorse bridge, nowadays known as Gallox Bridge, is first mentioned in written records in 1475. Present-day historians, however, believe that the bridge is much older than the first records show. In historical documents the name, earlier spelled as *Gallocksbrigge* or *Gallocks Bridge*, refers to what lay beyond it on Gallox Hill; the dreaded Dunster gallows, where hangings took place.

In medieval times it was common for the gallows to be placed at the entrance to towns like Dunster, reminding travellers of where they could end up if they did not obey the laws while passing through the settlements. The sight must have been terrifying, especially when the dead bodies of the convicted felons were displayed in iron cages, with crows feeding on the rotting flesh, no doubt adding to the superstitions surrounding the black birds of the Corvidae family.

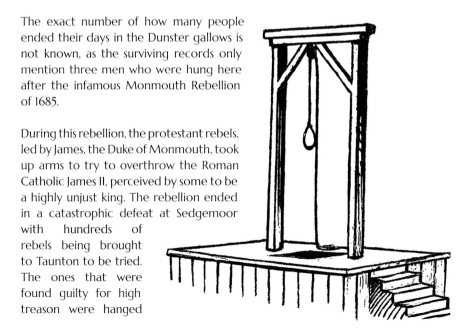

The exact number of how many people ended their days in the Dunster gallows is not known, as the surviving records only mention three men who were hung here after the infamous Monmouth Rebellion of 1685.

During this rebellion, the protestant rebels, led by James, the Duke of Monmouth, took up arms to try to overthrow the Roman Catholic James II, perceived by some to be a highly unjust king. The rebellion ended in a catastrophic defeat at Sedgemoor with hundreds of rebels being brought to Taunton to be tried. The ones that were found guilty for high treason were hanged and quartered in Taunton, with their heads and quarters boiled in salt and pitch - a process meant to preserve the body parts so they could be displayed in public places for a longer period of time.

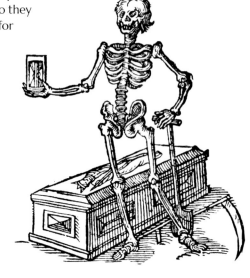

Besides executions, a great number of these unfortunate Somerset men were auctioned, and transported by ships to slavery in the West Indies. The survivors were granted a pardon after four years, but most of the wretched men didn't have the money to pay for the fare back home.

Records tell that the three Monmouth rebels that were sentenced to be hanged in Dunster, were led through the town with the locals gathered on the sides of the streets to watch the sad procession, no doubt either weeping and praying for the salvation of the mens' souls, or, if not closely acquainted with the men, wanting to touch the convicted men, as was the custom in the Middle Ages.

The medieval belief in the power of transference was particularly potent when the object was a convicted criminal. By laying one's hands on the felon, it was believed that whatever was ailing the townspeople, would be transferred onto the criminal and taken with him to hell.

The opposite was true, however, when it came to the touch of monarchs. It was believed that English kings and queens, the first recorded one being the Anglo-Saxon king Edward the Confessor (1042-1066), could cure scrofula, a type of a tuberculosis infection, just by touching the commoners affected by the disease. In later centuries, after being touched, the patient could also be given a pierced gold or silver coin, which would then be hung around the patient's neck, much in the same way as the amulets and ominous cures prescribed by the folk healers were.

To drive the message home of what could be expected if one were to rise against the God anointed king, the three rebels, one of them a Dunster based carpenter, were hanged and quartered in front of the townspeople on Gallox Hill, and the body parts placed at various public places around Dunster.

One of the GHOST STORIES told in Dunster is directly related to the historic event of convicts being taken to the Dunster gallows via Park Street. The story goes that a shadowy figure of a man, with his hands tied behind him, was seen walking on the corner of West Street and Park Street. The person telling the story to the author believed that the energy of traumatic events could get stored in the fabric of buildings, hence explaining why sensitive people could encounter such apparitions.

It was believed that monarchs could cure scrofula by just touching the infected people with their hands.

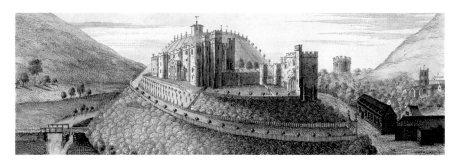

DUNSTER CASTLE

While the oldest parts of Dunster Castle date back to Norman times, the present-day interior is mainly the result of the remodelling done in the 17th and 19th centuries.

The castle has been inhabited by just two families, the de Mohuns, and the Luttrells, the latter of whom moved into the Castle in 1376, and left 600 years, and 21 generations later. In 1976, the castle was given to the National Trust.

The original owners, the de Mohuns, moved to Britain from France soon after 1066, when the Duke of Normandy, William the Conqueror, defeated the Anglo-Saxon army at the Battle of Hastings, and became the king of England. As a result, large amounts of land previously owned by the Anglo-Saxons were given to various French born, noble families.

William de Mohun built his timber castle in Dunster on a site, which is believed by some to previously have had an old Anglo-Saxon hill fort on it. Of the de Mohun's original castle only the 13th century lower level gateway, recognised by its impressive iron bound oak doors, remains to this day.

Just like most medieval British castles, Dunster Castle is home to many eerie stories passed down through generations.

THE STABLES

The early 17th century stabling building, which nowadays also houses a quaint National Trust shop, and can be found next to the main entrance to the castle, has several rather chilling stories told by both the staff and the visitors alike. A recurring one is of a life-like apparition of a man dressed in green clothes that appears from a wall, and disappears without a trace. The same GREEN MAN has been seen by the staff walking past the shop's glass doors, ignoring the staff's questions, only to disappear into nothing.

Another recent story tells of an elderly gentleman, who got the shock of his life, and was seen running out of the stables after seeing a man step out of the wall, right in front of him, and then, just like in the other stories, disappear without a trace. This apparition of a man is said to be sometimes accompanied by green orbs moving across the shop.

As if a clear apparition of a man was not enough, members of staff have also reported several incidents where boxes and displays in the shop have fallen without a warning, especially at the very end of the room, where the book shelves are currently located.

It is said that boxes have also been found in the store room containing dark coloured, sticky residue on the inner packets of the products meant to be sold in the shop, reminding the paranormal enthusiasts of *ectoplasm*, a substance believed to be left behind by ghosts. When the boxes were sent back to the supplier, the story goes, no explanation could be given as to what the residue was, or where it could have come from.

A recurring theme has also been of visitors telling staff of the strange, MENACING FEELING they have had in this building. The feeling has been especially strong around the far end of the stone built stables, with many wondering if someone might have been murdered here in the past.

Interestingly, there is actually a 17th century story of a castle servant, who went missing one night. The next morning a staff member came in to look at the horses, and found the missing servant's lifeless body lying on the floor, with a broken skull. The inquiry never led to anything, and to this day it is not known what happened that night at the stables.

Even the sceptics have been rattled in this building, as happened when a private ghost tour for Taunton-based office workers visited the stables. While the workers were joking about, and making ghostly sounds inside the stables, a lump of masonry, the size of a golf ball, fell down from the ceiling, and hit the end of one of the old wooden stalls. When the second one followed, the jokers went quiet, and, it is said, were rather relieved when it was time to leave the building.

THE OUBLIETTE

Next to the 13th century main gateway to the castle, in the right hand tower of the gatehouse, a seven metre deep oubliette containing several skeletons, was discovered during excavations performed in the 17th century.

An oubliette, a word derived from a French word *oublier*, meaning to forget, was a dungeon used in some medieval British castles as one of the horrific ways the medieval lords used to execute prisoners. The prisoners were thrown into a narrow cylindrical hole, with hardly any room to move around in, and left in the cold and dark to wait for their death, no doubt damaged by the long fall. Some had occasional food and water thrown in, but many were purely left to die, while standing on top of the bones of the earlier unfortunates.

The curious detail about Dunster Castle's 17th century excavations tells of one skeleton in particular, that was highly unusual for the time. The skeleton was manacled by wrists and ankles to the wall of the oubliette, and was measured to be the remains of a 2.20 metre (7.2 ft) tall man. When an average height for a man in those days was around 1.5 metres (4.9 ft), this man must have been considered a giant compared to the other townspeople.

With such a horrendous history, it is no wonder that there are stories of strange sounds and cries coming from the direction of the oubliette, nowadays covered with a concrete roof. Stories also talk of dogs, that refuse to go up the steps next to the tower.

THE CRYPT

Visitors also talk of the Crypt, which was used as a dungeon during the 17th century Civil War, as being especially unnerving.

A castle staff member told the author a story of a couple, who, while visiting the Crypt, all of a sudden saw a strange mist form in front of them. While they looked on, the mist took the form of faces and bodies with hands reaching out towards them. The couple told the staff member that when they heard a whisper, '*Get out you have done enough*', they turned around and left the Crypt as quickly as they could.

Another common story told of the castle is that of several visitors feeling sick as soon as they enter the main building. One visitor told the staff that as her visit went on, the feeling and her headache, got worse. When she finally reached the Crypt, she felt somebody touch her hair. She thought it was her friend who was with her at the time, but the friend swore that she hadn't touched her. As the friend walked away, the visitor felt her hair touched again.

A similar sort of sensation of a contact in the Crypt was experienced by another female visitor to the castle. While she was standing in the doorway of the Crypt, she felt as if somebody was pushing her away from the door. Her dog started barking, and then she felt another push. She quickly took her dog, and left the doorway.

GRISEL GRIS

An ancient story based around the same area, the entrance to the castle, is that of the mighty warhorse Grisel Gris.

Trained war horses were deadly opponents on the battle fields, and worth a great deal of money to medieval knights. This massive, grey horse was given to Sir John de Mohun V, the Lord of Dunster Castle at that time, by Edward the Black Prince, for his bravery on the battle field.

The unfortunate incident involving this pride and joy of his master, unfolded on one icy cold winter day on the steep road leading down from the castle to the gateway. Sir John was training his other horses, and whistled to Grisel Gris who was eating grass on the castle yard. Recognising his master's call, Grisel Gris galloped down the steep road, but slipped, fell, and hit his head on the wall, dying on the spot.

Perhaps because of this 700-year-old story, or the centuries of horses having been ridden up and down Castle Hill, there are several reports of people having heard the sounds of hooves in this area in the night, when no horses were around. Some stories also talk of an apparition of a grand ghostly stallion, believed to be the unfortunate Grisel Gris.

PARTIAL APPARITIONS

Dunster Castle's kitchen is the site of a more recent story where a male volunteer was sent to clean the room. While he was brushing the floor, he saw a naked foot materialise out of thin air, between the two kitchen doorways. He described the foot as being almost transparent, but as though covered in white powder, fading out completely at the ankle. The foot took one step forward, and then disappeared. The young man, the story goes, fled from the room, badly shaken by the experience.

Another encounter in the same kitchen talks of a drop in temperature, and a mist forming in the corner, in the middle of which an apparition of a man appeared.

A similar story about a partial apparition, is the one told of a face appearing in the old Servants' Room. This room used to be very busy in its day, but nowadays, for some reason, gives chills to the visitors, the staff, and the tradespeople working in this part of the castle.

THE LEATHER GALLERY

The most troubled part of the castle, though, if judged by the number of stories told about it, is the Leather Gallery, named after the rare, painted leather wall hangings seen here, depicting the story of Antony and Cleopatra.

The Leather Gallery used to form part of the medieval castle's Great Hall, which extended through to what is now the Property Manager's apartment. The stories talk of sightings in the Gallery and the surrounding rooms, the sounds of heavy steps, slamming of doors, loud shouts, and a feeling of being tapped on the shoulder in broad daylight. There are also stories of sightings of foot guards wearing tricorn hats, cold spots, and both the staff and the visitors experiencing feelings of distinct unease.

In the 1990s, when a staff member's mother was staying overnight in a room close to the Leather Gallery, and reading a book in the evening, it is said that she heard male voices coming from the Gallery. Thinking it was her son, she asked about it the next morning only to find out that neither her son, nor anyone else, had been in the Gallery. On the same night, the staff member's partner and her brother had been startled by the same sounds of men talking, footsteps, and a door banging. Staying in two separate rooms, neither had had the courage to go and have a look, but the next morning, while recounting the previous night's incidents, found that they had both heard the same sounds at the exact same time, adding on to the other visitors' stories of similar incidents in the same area.

Another, 1950s story talks of two tradesmen who were sent to the Leather Gallery to lift the floorboards up, so that the heating pipes under the floor could be accessed. While working on the floor, the story goes, both men felt an acute sense of terror, with the young apprentice feeling physically sick. When they left the room, they immediately felt better. The apprentice refused to go back in the room, and another workman was sent to finish the job. He didn't feel anything, and the work was completed.

In the same Leather Gallery, a staff member is said to have all of a sudden felt the temperature drop. It was a hot day, and while polishing the floors, she had a feeling that somebody was standing behind her. She turned around, and much to her surprise, saw a figure of a man standing in the doorway, wearing an old-fashioned military uniform. She said that when the figure disappeared, the room temperature returned to normal.

There is also a story that talks of a male visitor in his forties feeling a strong sense of unease as soon as he walked through the castle's main doorway. He had pushed the feeling aside, told his wife to go ahead, but while walking up the stairs towards the Leather Gallery by himself, felt something push him back, as if he wasn't allowed to go further. The man was so badly shaken, the former staff member recounts, that he had to go and wait for his wife in the conservatory, and as soon as she arrived, they left the castle.

The room where the Prince of Wales, later to become King Charles II, stayed in 1645, is also right next to the Leather Gallery. It is told that during the young prince's two week stay at Dunster Castle, he would wake up on several nights to claim that there was a ghostly apparition in the room. A present-day staff member also told a story of a visitor who refused to leave this same room, called King Charles's bedroom, because he was terrified of the pool of blood he saw in the doorway, and which he didn't want to walk through.

A local medium told the author about the experience she had when they moved to the area. While in the Leather Gallery she suddenly encountered an apparition of a soldier dressed in WWII uniform. *"The apparition was so vivid, that I thought it was someone dressed up in an old uniform. I found out later that during the Second World War, the castle had doubled up as a hospital unit for the recuperation of the soldiers returning from the war."*

A similar apparition of a soldier has been seen by other visitors as well, prior to a sudden change in temperature. This area, the story goes, besides being used for the rehabilitation of WWII soldiers, was also used as a dormitory for Civil War troops in the mid-seventeenth century.

THE GREY LADY

Other frequent stories of an apparition encountered in Dunster Castle are those told of the Grey Lady. She has been sighted in different parts of the castle, in the Library, the Billiard Room, the staircases, and the corridors. Many of the stories place her gliding gracefully up and down the old oak staircase, a place where many of the castle's staff, it is said, not only have felt a great sense of unease, but also have found the banisters oddly wet to the touch.

The Grey Lady has also made one memorable appearance on the Servants' Staircase. A staff member recalls the story of a man coming away from the staircase, white as a sheet, and saying that while he was walking down the stairs, she saw a girl dressed in old-fashioned clothes. The girl had said to him: *"I just need to go"*, so the visitor walked downstairs with the girl. When they reached the bottom, the Grey Lady appeared, and he heard her say to the girl: *"Oh, there you are, do come along"*, before they both disappeared. The man, the story goes, was very badly shaken.

The frequent encounters with the Grey Lady troubled the staff so much that at one point an exorcist was called in to rid the castle of the apparition. The exorcist claimed to have found the presence of several spirits on the staircase and the Drawing Room below. She had asked the spirits to leave, and believed that they had.

THE HAUNTED PIANO

Another recent story told of Dunster Castle is that of an incident involving a piano playing by itself. While walking around the castle a group of staff members were startled to hear the distinct notes of a piano being played. When they heard the sounds again, the story goes, they rushed into the room where the piano was, only to find that no one was there. This is said to have happened on several occasions, with some of the staff stating that they had also seen sheets of music fly across the room. When investigated, they found all the windows shut, thus concluding that the sheets could not have flown up because of a draught.

A GHOST VOLUNTEER

Besides the full-time staff members, the National Trust owned Dunster Castle is nowadays maintained by a great number of volunteers who, through their kind efforts, help to keep its ancient doors open to visitors.

The last one of the fascinating tales collected for this book involves one of these volunteers, a former Room Steward who used to be stationed at the Inner Hall. This kind lady was absolutely devoted to the castle and is said to have loved telling her stories to the enchanted visitors.

Unfortunately the Room Steward was struck down with an illness, and eventually passed away. Since her departure, however, several visitors have told the staff members of their encounters with an apparition of an elderly lady sitting peacefully in the Steward's chair in the Inner Hall, and who, when approached, would disappear right in front of the visitors' eyes.

Whether the apparition is the departed Room Steward, or not, the story certainly deserves its place in the long line of fascinating tales told of this beautiful castle, and the surrounding village of Dunster. It also reminds readers that not all ghost stories are something to be frightened of. People have enjoyed telling and re-telling otherworldly stories for thousands of years, and hopefully, will continue to do so for many years to come.

After all, there is still so much in this world that cannot be explained, and if stories like the ones recounted in this book bring a little bit of magic and wonder to our everyday lives, the stories should be enjoyed, and keep on being shared.

THE AUTHOR & THE ILLUSTRATOR

THE AUTHOR

Nina Dodd is a photographer and a journalist, who has been living in the Exmoor area since 2011. Born in Helsinki, Finland, she did her Master's degree in English Literature with Joint Honours in Journalism, Cultural History, Comparative Religions, East-Asian Studies and Pedagogics. She has also completed a four year course in photography, and is a qualified, professional photographer. While living in Finland, Nina wrote articles and did photo assignments for 15 years for Finland's largest newspapers and magazines, before deciding to concentrate mainly on photography. Nina has travelled extensively and lived - besides the UK and Finland - in Japan, the US, and Canada, where she worked for a Canadian-Finnish newspaper.

Nina's interest in otherworldly phenomena was born early, as she was brought up with stories of the supernatural. Her mother, aunt and grandmother, not only believed in ghosts, but believed to have had first-hand encounters. Nina describes herself as *"slightly sceptical with an open mind"*, even though she does admit to having had encounters that could be classed as *'otherworldly'.*

Nina lives in Dunster with her British husband and their two sons, does photo shoots, and owns a Scandinavian-British lifestyle shop Dunster Living.

THE ILLUSTRATOR

Asia Wetherell is a digital artist with a Bachelor of Arts degree in Digital Media from the Australian National University. Asia's designs have been featured on a wide range of products from greeting cards to clothing. In addition to her own creative projects, Asia has also worked extensively as a website and digital media contractor for the Australian government. In 2015 Asia and her artist husband Tim moved to the northern shores of Exmoor, where they run an arts business.

The illustrations for this book were digitally created by Asia utilising Asia's and Nina's own drawings and photographs, and digital adaptations of historic public domain drawings and paintings.

Having had a few ghostly encounters herself, Asia was excited to be involved in creating a book about local superstitions, beliefs and otherworldly encounters.

BIBLIOGRAPHY & FURTHER READING

- A Book of Exmoor, F.J. Snell (Halsgrove, 2002)
- A People Bewitched - *Witchcraft and Magic in Nineteenth-Century Somerset*, Owen Davies (Owen Davies, 1999)
- A Natural History of Ghosts - *500 Years of Hunting for Proof*, Roger Clark Penguin Books, 2013)
- An Archaeological Assessment of Dunster, English Heritage Extensive Urban Survey, Clare Gathercole (Somerset County Council)
- Blood and Mistletoe - *The History of the Druids in Britain*, Ronald Hutton (Yale University Press, 2022)
- Discovering Dunster - *A History and Guide*, Hilary Binding (Halsgrove, 1990)
- Dunster - A Castle at War, Jim Lee (Mereo, 2014)
- Dunster Priory, Dunster, Somerset - Dig Village Evaluations - Tim Darch (2014)
- Ghosts in the Middle Ages, Jean-Claude Schmitt (The University of Chicago Press, 1998)
- Ghosts - *Mysterious Tales from the National Trust*, Siân Evans (HarperCollins Publishers, 2006)
- History of Britain & Ireland (Dorling Kindersley Limited, 2011)
- Hope Bourne's History of Exmoor, Hope L. Bourne (Halsgrove, 2018)
- Legends of Exmoor, Jack Hurley (The Exmoor Press, 1988)
- Magical House Protection, Brian Hoggard (Berghahn Books, 2021)
- Medieval Graffiti, Matthew Champion (Ebury Press, 2015)
- Pagan Britain, Ronald Hutton (Yale University Press, 2014)
- Shoes Concealed in Buildings, Northampton Museum Journal 6 (December 1969), Swann, J.M.
- The Book of English Magic, Philip Carr-Comm, Richard Heygate (John Murray, 2009)
- The First Ghosts, Irving Finkel (Hodder & Stoughton, 2022)
- The Ghost Story 1840-1920 - *A cultural history*, Andrew Smith (Manchester University Press, 2012)
- The History of Dunster Church and Priory, Joan Jordan (Halsgrove, 2007)

- The History of Witchcraft and Demonology, Montague Summers (Castle Books, 1992)
- The Ladies of Dunster Castle, Jim Lee (Mereo Books, 2016)
- The Secret Middle Ages, Malcolm Jones (Sutton Publishing, 2002)
- The Shortest History of England, James Hawes (Old Street Publishing, 2021)
- The Witch - *A History of Fear, From Ancient Times To the Present*, Ronald Hutton (Yale University Press, 2018)
- The Witches of Selwood - *Witchcraft Belief and Accusation in Seventeenth-Century Somerset*, Andrew Pickering (The Hobnob Press, 2021)
- Unearthing Dunster - Time Team Digital Dig Village Project 2012-2018, Stewart Ainsworth, John Allan, Richard Parker, Tim Taylor
- West Country Superstitions, an article in The South Australian Advertiser newspaper, 15 June 1870, page 3.
- Witchcraft - *A Secret History,* Michael Streeter (White Lion Publishing, 2020)
- Witch, Wicce, Mother Goose, Robert W. Thurston (Pearson Education, 2001)
- Witchcraft in the Modern World - New Perspectives on Witchcraft, Magic and Demonology, Brian P. Levack (editor) (Routledge, 2001)

- ONLINE
- academia.edu (Dunster Priory, Dunster, Somerset - Dig Village Evaluations)
- ancient-yew.org
- apotropaios.co.uk
- arch.cam.ac.uk (Rings, Kings, Saints and Toads, Róisín Donohoe)
- BBC documentary Lucy Worsley investigates, Series 1:1 The Witch Hunts, series 1:2. The Black Death
- BBC Story of England 1-6, Michael Woods
- britannica.com
- british-history.ac.uk
- britishlistedbuildings.co.uk
- dunsterancestors.co.uk
- english-heritage.org.uk
- exmoorher.co.uk
- faeryfolklorist.blogspot.com
- historicengland.org.uk (Disease in the Middle Ages, Ellen Castelow,)

- historic-uk.com
- historyfiles.co.uk/KingListsBritain/BritainDumnonia
- history.rcplondon.ac.uk/blog/touching-kings-evil-short-history
- hoxnehistory.org.uk (Witch marks of Hoxne)
- medievalists.net
- ncbi.nlm.nih.gov (Medical Magic and the Church in Thirteenth Century England, Catherine Rider)
- nursingclio.org (Weaving Wool into Death, Kim Barrett)
- pans.org (Acceleration of plague outbreaks in the second pandemic, David J.D. Earn)
- rakinglight.co.uk
- sans.org/early-dunster-project
- shura.shu.ac.uk (Marks of the Witch: Britain's ritual protection symbols, David Clarke)
- somersetheritage.org.uk
- world history.org (Sacred Sites & Rituals in the Ancient Celtic Religion, Mark Cartwright)
- youtube.com (Dig village Dunster video blogs)
- britishnewspaperarchive.co.uk

- IMAGE CREDIT
- Page 12: Virgin Mary illumination from the British Library (https://www.bl.uk)

HAVE
YOU GOT
A STORY
TO TELL?

Collecting local ghost stories and folktales is an ongoing project for the author, so if you have a story to tell involving Dunster, or any other areas in and around Exmoor,

please email them to:
dunsterbooks@gmail.com

or send them by post to:
Dunster Books
30 High Street
Dunster, Somerset TA24 6SG

Please include your contact details, so if need be, you can be contacted for further details.

THANK YOU!